LEAD
TO
WIN

How to Be a Powerful, Impactful,

Influential Leader in Any Environment

Carla A. Harris

Avery
an imprint of Penguin Random House
New York

AVERY

an imprint of Penguin Random House LLC
penguinrandomhouse.com

Most Avery books are available at special quantity discounts for bulk purchase for sales promotions, premiums, fund-raising, and educational needs. Special books or book excerpts also can be created to fit specific needs. For details, write SpecialMarkets@penguinrandomhouse.com.

Library of Congress Cataloging-in-Publication Data

Names: Harris, Carla A., author.
Title: Lead to win: how to be a powerful, impactful, influential leader
in any environment / Carla A. Harris.
Description: New York: Avery, [2022]
Identifiers: LCCN 2022005292 (print) | LCCN 2022005293 (ebook) |
ISBN 9780593421680 (hardcover) | ISBN 9780593421697 (epub)
Subjects: LCSH: Leadership. | Executive ability. | Success in business.
Classification: LCC HD57.7 .H36936 2022 (print) |
LCC HD57.7 (ebook) | DDC 658.4/092—dc23/eng/20220202
LC record available at https://lccn.loc.gov/2022005292
LC ebook record available at https://lccn.loc.gov/2022005293

Printed in the United States of America
2nd Printing

Book design by Patrice Sheridan

To my daughters, Dakota and McKinley

May you realize and become the great leader
that is already inside of you

CONTENTS

Introduction

DURING MY THREE-PLUS decades as an investment banker on Wall Street, I've worked side by side with colleagues, served on numerous boards, volunteered my time with countless nonprofits, and traveled the world coaching and speaking. In that time, I've executed hundreds of deals and had the opportunity to work closely with and observe countless CEOs from a wide range of industries, including technology, retail, transportation, industrial, and healthcare, to name a few. As a result, in good economies and bad, I was exposed to and had the opportunity to study some great leaders . . . and some not-so-great leaders. I have also observed some very effective leadership styles as well as seen the results of some incredibly ineffective approaches, too.

In all I've seen, there is one factor that stands out. Most of those leaders, CEOs and other executives, never received any extended formal training or coaching on how to be a great leader. Further, most lead in the same way they were led during their careers, often using the "my way or the highway" approach.

During the decades of the 1980s and 1990s, and frankly, for the thirty years before then, it was an organization's leaders who defined its agenda. They called the shots and decided what needed to happen and when. Further, every professional who worked for them was expected to do exactly as they dictated, no questions asked. In this

paradigm, leaders often managed by fear and threats. If you didn't execute in the way defined by the leader or behave as the culture demanded, you could be demoted, left in a dead-end job, or worse, be
fired. Under a leader like this, you would never have the opportunity
to disagree or offer any input or constructive feedback. Essentially, you
did as you were told.

For a time, this "my way or the highway" leadership style was
considered impactful and effective. There was no war for talent in this
period, and production and volume were valued over innovation, con-
venience, and price. Today's environment is different. Innovation is the
dominant competitive parameter; speed to market of new products and
the ability to directly engage consumers follow closely behind and are
the table stakes for competition and survival in the marketplace.

What's also different today is that, at the time of this writing, we
find ourselves more than a year and a half into a global pandemic. Many
workers have had the opportunity to work from home or from some
other remote location of their choosing, instead of an office building.
A challenging time for most people, the time in lockdown has also offered employees the opportunity to reflect on their lives and consider
their career choices. They are asking themselves questions such as "Am
I in the right job?" "Am I pursuing a career that makes me happy?"
"Does my employer or my boss treat me well?"

This level of reflection without the reinforcement that comes from
being close to colleagues and managers has some employees, at a minimum, considering why they are with a certain employer, and many
others contemplating leaving their current jobs. I believe the consequence of this contemplation will be a great shift of employees from
one employer to another, or from corporate or philanthropic work to
entrepreneurship. As a result, employers are being forced to re-evaluate
their value proposition for workers to engage with them and will have
to market that proposition in the marketplace in a way that will help
them retain their best talent and attract new workers.

In addition, I believe that companies will have to rethink how they reward and compensate people who are very effective at not only attracting great talent but retaining it, which is very different from the way companies have rewarded people heretofore. In most industries, especially financial services, if you are a great producer, generating millions of dollars of revenue, you are generally the highest-paid person, while people who are heralded as great managers—whose teams love them and who tend to be great developers of people, so their teams stay with the company—are not valued and rewarded in the same way. Well, in today's environment, with companies having the new awakening about its people, employers will have to value those who can lead and manage differently than in the past, more like the way they reward traditional "producers."

Institutions are increasingly beginning to value and depend on collaborative alliances versus proprietary ideas and products. Technology has changed the game and taught other industries the value of open sourcing and partnerships. As a result, companies can no longer rely solely on their own internal talent to compete, let alone lead. To forge partnerships, attract collaborators and foster relationships, and, more important, attract and retain the best talent, you need to be a different kind of leader. If you are going to motivate and inspire talented professionals to choose to spend their time within the walls of your company, to have a muscle of innovation, you have to be able to engage, penetrate thought, teach, and inspire. To lead in today's business and philanthropic world requires you to have the courage to be authentic, build trust, focus on diversity, and be resilient and tenacious.

Past leaders, corporate leaders in particular, had three constituents to worry about: shareholders, customers, and employees. Now a fourth constituent has emerged and is a major focus . . . community. Armed with and emboldened by social media, the community can use this powerful tool to, in minutes, take down a brand franchise that took decades to build. With the ongoing pressure on organizations to constantly innovate, given geopolitical uncertainty, cybersecurity threats, social media, and the war for talent, the pressures on leaders seem endless. Even if an organization has developed a rock-solid competitive strategy and its balance sheet is solid, there are ongoing threats to its culture, such as the repercussions of a bad actor, a leadership scandal, or a lapse in judgment that results in threats from activist groups or damage to a customer relationship.

So what does it take to lead effectively today? As a leader, how do you stay vigilant? How do you maintain your energy to stay the course? How can you be successful amidst the many pressures and threats?

In this book, I will discuss the journey to leadership and some of the essential skills you need for success, including the importance of taking risks, creating a vision, and leveraging assets like relationships and partnerships. At the heart of this book are my ten pearls of Intentional Leadership:

#1 Leadership is a journey from execution to empowerment.

#2 How people feel about you as a leader will impact how they perform and what they deliver.

#3 Choosing the right team will define your legacy.

#4 Fear has no place in your success equation. Leaders take risks to grow.

#5 No one can do it alone. Leveraging other people's intellect, relationships, and experience as well as establishing your own relationships will propel your success as a leader.

#6 You are not a leader because you have the title; you must be intentional.

#7 Leading today requires the ability to transform . . . people, situations, and yourself.

#8 Visibility, transparency, decisiveness, and empathy will help you to lead effectively through a crisis.

#9 Everyone has a blind spot. Identify yours and make it a priority to eliminate it.

#10 Strong insight will lead you to focus on and execute what will be instead of what is.

These are attributes that you need to focus on and exhibit to become a powerful, impactful leader no matter where you work.

Finally, I will discuss the attributes of an intentional leader, the key traits of being a transformational leader, and the gaps that I have seen in leadership that could impede or damage any leader's effectiveness. You do not automatically become a leader because one day you are given a title or position of authority and responsibility. Leadership is active. To be successful, I believe you have to show up and focus on being an intentional leader every day.

In producer cultures, like finance, technology, and sales and marketing, people are rewarded with not only outsize compensation but also promotions, titles, and positions of authority. There is little thought given to whether they have the skills and ability to coach, motivate, and inspire others to deliver beyond what they believe they can. Yet, that is exactly the kind of leader who is needed in today's competitive environment.

The great Billie Jean King is credited with the quote "Pressure is a privilege." There is no question that if you choose to accept a leadership position and sit in the leadership seat, you will have pressure. Pressure to lead effectively, pressure to make the organization better than you found it, and pressure to be a value add to the people who work in the organization.

I believe it is a privilege to lead. In *Lead to Win*, I will deliver the tools you need to be a powerful, impactful leader who can lead from any seat and lead to win.

CHAPTER 1

Moving from Individual Contributor to Leader

LEADERSHIP PEARL #1
Leadership is a journey from execution to empowerment.

YOU ARE READING this book because you aspire to be a leader. When you begin your career it's typically in an entry-level role as an individual contributor. Your duties are assigned; your specific actions are dictated. Your job is to understand and execute any assignment you are given. In other words, your job is to DO, not to DEFINE, and to execute EXACTLY as instructed.

There will be times when you are given an assignment and are expected to add your own style. Other times, you will be asked to perform using a hybrid approach, doing some of what you were asked to do and some of what you decide is necessary. But for the most part, as an individual contributor, your focus is on achieving a previously defined outcome. Your performance review will likely focus less on the process and more on how well or how closely you followed the instructions you were given. In short, how well did you get the job done?

As an individual contributor, you are also generally not responsible for managing or leading other people. Typically, no one reports to you, you don't have to assign tasks to others, nor are you responsible for their coaching or professional development. You are not concerned with managing resources, optimizing people, or considering the concerns or needs of external constituents.

While your work or contribution is important to the company and may even be essential to the profitability and competitiveness of the organization, your reward is tied solely to what you produce. You are given the resources you need to accomplish what you are responsible for. You are not concerned with balancing the needs of shareholders, employees, customers, senior leadership, or other stakeholders. Your job is to create an outcome.

As you enjoy more success as an individual contributor, you will start to develop a strong, positive reputation. People in leadership positions will start to notice you and begin to consider you a leadership candidate. Your company will begin to inquire about your interest in advancing to a leadership position. In most organizations, after it appears you have mastered your role as an individual contributor, managing other people is the next step. Part of the assessment of your readiness for a leadership role focuses on whether you have exhibited leadership attributes while in your individual contributor seat: Have you demonstrated that you can take initiative, do you know how to recognize and take advantage of opportunities, do you have the ability to build relationships, and are you comfortable taking risks?

Leadership is a journey from execution to empowerment. As a leader, you go from getting the job done to focusing on giving others the tools, the resources, the experiences, and the opportunities they need to develop and evolve their own leadership skills. While there certainly might be tasks and decisions that only you as the leader must make, your time as a leader should be filled with anticipating the needs of those working with you and those of the customers, constituents, and other stakeholders your actions serve.

As you are advancing along your career journey, it is important that while you execute your assignments, you also look for opportunities to lead. Often those who are evaluating you are looking for signs of your ability to lead or for signs that you have an appetite or aspiration to lead.

It is important that *you* take the initiative to seek out these opportunities because those above you will not always tell you that you are being observed and assessed for potential leadership opportunities. Part of the "test" used to assess your leadership capabilities includes how much initiative you demonstrate in your day-to-day work and whether you can recognize opportunities to lead, as well as take advantage of them.

Allyson had been working on the presentation for a new marketing idea for one of her firm's largest clients. This was an idea that could significantly enhance the effectiveness of the client's digital marketing campaign. It was a lucrative contract for the firm, and the project had a compressed go to market deadline. Every assignment before the pilot of the new program had been tightly controlled and dictated by the partner on the team. While Allyson had been working with this client on various projects for over a year and had a great relationship with her counterpart at the client as well as with their senior officers, all communication with the client had previously gone through the senior partner on her team.

Allyson finished the project and thought she had put together an outstanding solution. She really wanted to get a sense of whether it would receive a positive reaction from the client. Her inclination was to call her counterpart there to get an "off the record" reaction before moving forward with the recommendation. But she recognized that while it might show initiative, it might anger the senior partner, who could perceive her as going around his back. On the other hand, she thought it would demonstrate strong forward thinking and initiative and might give them the opportunity before the meeting to use informal feedback to refine their approach if necessary.

Allyson decided to call her counterpart, who gave her significant feedback, prompting her to completely overhaul their original solution. When the team went in to present, the client loved the recommendations and gave them the contract. When Allyson's boss asked her how she had developed an idea that was so closely aligned with the client's objectives when they had received so little guidance, she told him, with some trepidation, about the "off the record" call. Allyson decided to be transparent because she knew that transparency is one of the keys to building trust. Her boss had clearly trusted her up to this point. She did not want to impair that trust. In fact, she hoped it would grow if she told him exactly what she had done.

Allyson was thrilled when her boss praised her for having the idea and the initiative to get the preliminary feedback and to work with the client to produce a product they were excited about. At the end of the year, as the partners were discussing promotion candidates, this incident was used as an example of Allyson's readiness to be promoted to a leadership role in the department. Why? First, she showed her ability to take a calculated risk. Second, she demonstrated her relationship skills by leveraging a contact to get valuable information. Third, she showed she could take initiative by changing the presentation. All these attributes are similar to those expected of a leader.

Now let's imagine that Allyson had played it safe and decided not to follow her instincts and risk the ire of the partner. Allyson's team would have gone with the original presentation and would not have received the same effusive praise from the client. Further, they might not have been awarded the contract or, at a minimum, would have opened the door to competition. In addition, there would have been no example of Allyson exhibiting three of the four major characteristics sought in a leader—risk-taking, initiative, and the ability to approach, collaborate with, and innovate with clients. When the partner discussion turned toward Allyson's capacity or readiness to lead, the outcome would have been unclear at best.

Your ability to take advantage of leadership opportunities is a critical step on the journey to becoming a leader. There is no question that there are risks involved. You could misidentify an opportunity. You might risk "blowback," upsetting a superior who may feel that you are overstepping or challenging their decision-making authority. You also risk that you may fumble the chance, or risk that the outcome is not what you thought it would be. However, in my experience, the benefit of stepping up to demonstrate your leadership capacity is always far greater than the risk of things going awry.

LEADERSHIP GEM:

Leadership is not about always being right but about having the courage to take a risk, move forward, maintain momentum, and, if you fail, try again.

If your job as an individual contributor is to *do* according to the expectations of others, your job as a leader is to *define* a project's objective, goals, and outcome while setting clear expectations for others and maximizing the use of the resources (people, financial, and technological) at hand. You are responsible for identifying potential gaps and challenges and minimizing any potential risks to the process, the outcome, and the organization. While you may also be involved in the execution, your primary responsibility will be to develop the agenda, determine what needs to be done, who will execute and do the work, and sometimes even how and when the work will get done.

As you transition to a role as a leader, it is important that you adopt a macro view of your organization. You will need to learn about things such as how budgets are created, how resources are allocated, who makes resource allocation decisions, who the organization's other strong performers are, and who the stakeholders are. In addition to deciding what needs to be done, part of your role as a leader is to understand how your project fits in with the organization's other priorities, as well as which resources are required and costs are associated with what you are trying to accomplish. Understanding the kinds of resources you need and the associated costs of a project are key to developing efficient assignments and agendas.

One of the great leaders in my firm would always say, "Think like an owner." This gave me the sense that once I became a leader, I had to think about considerations such as shareholder value. This not only meant revenue maximization but profit maximization and therefore cost minimization. In my endeavor to get a job done, I also had to be mindful of properly using resources and not wasting them.

It is never too early to start learning about some of the things that the leaders in your organization are responsible for. Because as you progress and can demonstrate an understanding of even a few of these things, it will create a perception that you are interested in becoming a senior leader yourself. In addition, the converse can be true. If you do not show such interest, others will perceive it to mean that either you are not interested in rising in the organization or you are not leadership material.

In the early days of my career, I believe this failure to demonstrate curiosity about the things that were "above my pay grade" contributed to a negative perception about me. I will admit that I was far too myopic, focusing *only* on those things that were clearly a part of the junior associate's job. I was so focused on mastering those tasks that I failed to realize that it was important to demonstrate my interest in understanding the concepts that were beyond my junior associate's role, and the positive impression that could be created by doing so.

I was working in mergers and acquisitions (M&A) at the time. One of the important components of an M&A deal is the fee letter. This letter outlines the terms and conditions between the M&A advisor (the investment bank) and the client that is retaining the services of the bank. The letter not only informs the client what the bank will charge for completing the transaction; it also contains important deal concepts like indemnifications, termination fees, the tasks that are involved in executing the deal, and any contingent or extra fees that could be earned.

During my second year as an associate, the managing director asked me to draft a fee letter. I didn't have a clue what he was talking about! Of course, I could deduce what he meant from the term *fee letter*, but I had no idea where to start, where to find a draft of one, how to take a stab at what the fee might be for such a transaction, or anything else, for that matter. Throughout my first year as an associate, no one had ever explained to me what the key components were, nor had I ever asked. I had kept my head down, producing models and analysis, but had never stopped to look up to understand what was involved. I had no idea how we got the transaction, what happened after the firm was awarded the business, and how and when we would negotiate the transaction's price.

I focused solely on my small part. When I started asking questions about what a fee letter was and how to write one, it was clear from the expression on my managing director's face that he was surprised and disappointed that as a second-year associate, I did not understand one of the most important components of the deal. Further, that I did not have an understanding or even demonstrate curiosity about how we got paid! Needless to say, after that experience, I made it my business to learn all the key parts of a fee letter, including the nuances or special circumstances that would cause the firm to adjust fees up or down. While I never made that mistake again, clearly, I had to work hard to change the perception about me and my career trajectory, my interest in moving ahead, and my capacity as a leader in the eyes of that managing director.

SELLING THE VISION

A great leader creates the vision they want others to follow. They create an argument to sell it to others, making it attractive and compelling to those who must approve it as well as to those who need to embrace and act upon it. To sell an idea, you must consider why the idea is great for the department, the organization, or the people who are involved. You will need to answer questions such as:

- Why should the organization do this?
- How does the organization benefit from taking on this project?
- How do the customers benefit?
- Do the employees or shareholders benefit?
- Does it make a current process more efficient?
- Does it save resources?
- Does it serve or help more people?
- Does this new product or process put the organization in a position to lead in its vertical or its industry?
- Does it make the organization more competitive?

It is important to note, every project or endeavor that you bring to your team or organization has a beneficiary, and that beneficiary has to be greater than you. As a leader, you must always consider how your decisions impact others. Ideally, whatever idea you are proposing is scalable and will benefit a large number of customers, shareholders, or employees. I cannot think of one successful leadership vision that did not favorably impact others.

LEADERSHIP GEM:

Every leadership vision, idea, and decision will impact others.

Whether you are a teacher, preacher, coach, CEO of a public company or a not-for-profit, COO, CFO, shift manager, supervisor, manager, mayor, governor, or Congressperson, no one in authority makes a decision in a vacuum. Every decision you make in your capacity as a leader will affect someone else. The questions are: Who will be impacted and how? Will they win or lose? Does it improve the organization or threaten it? Will it make people, inside and outside the organization, better off? Will it make people's jobs harder, more interesting, or easier? Every decision you make has an impact. That is the nature of leadership.

How do you develop the vision for your idea? The inspiration you need for deciding how to move your organization forward is all around you. If things are going well for your organization, your inspiration can come from questions like:

- What can we do to create greater value for our shareholders, i.e., an increased stock price, greater dividend yield?
- What can we do to improve our market share relative to the competition?
- What can we do to improve our competitive advantage or to create a new one?
- What can we do to preserve the company's leadership status going forward?
- How can we serve our customers better?
- How can we make life better for our employees?
- If we were starting the company today, what would we do differently?
- What legacy practices have caused us to do things the way we do them today? How might we change that?
- What partnerships should we seek to better leverage our strengths or move into a new area?

If your company is having a tough time competitively, your vision might be inspired by questions like:

- How can we turn around our competitive performance?
- How can we create an environment where our best people will want to stay or attract others to work here?

- How can we change the narrative about our trajectory?
- How can we convince our stakeholders to trust us again?
- What businesses need the greatest investment?
- How do I prioritize our current needs as a company?
- Have I properly allocated resources to the areas of the business that need it most?
- Should I consider a partnership with a competitor or another entity?
- Should we build to be more competitive or should we buy?
- Should we do an "acqui-hire" of a disruptive emerging company's management team?

In general, your vision as a leader can be inspired by the competition, by a desire to do what is best for your employees, for your company's survival, and for ensuring its future. Notice that none of the preceding questions is relevant to who *you* are as one person or what *you* can individually gain, but rather to what can be done to increase the value for the current shareholders or employees or for those constituencies in the future. If your vision is solely driven by your personal benefit, then it will be constrained by your own capabilities or fears.

If you are a CEO, your board of directors will look to you to develop and deliver a strategic plan that will drive maximum value for shareholders, given the competitive environment and a finite set of financial, technological, physical, and human resources. While the board may have a perspective on what should be done to enhance shareholder value, they will look to you for your thoughts on what should be done, the execution timeline, the resources needed, the risks involved, and the answer to the question "What could go wrong?" If you are a leader within an organization, the CEO will look to you to develop a vision for executing a portion of the strategic plan and to answer those same questions as they pertain to your part of the plan.

If you are a CEO of a private company, a college president, or a leader of a nonprofit organization, your board, trustees, or board of advisors will also expect you to define the vision for the organization's future. They want to see you demonstrate that you are a good steward of the assets that have been entrusted to you. In the case of a private company, especially an early-stage company, investors will look closely at your track record of deploying the capital you have raised to produce greater value for the company.

If your company has not increased in its valuation from one raise to the next and there is not an exogenous market occurrence that has impacted the companies in that sector, then it will be difficult for you to raise additional rounds of funding because you did not use the money from the previous round wisely. If as a college president you can't demonstrate that you have deployed the capital raised to attract more students or bring on more renowned scholars, or produced research or products that are leveraged by for-profit entities, then it will compromise your standing as a leader at that institution.

As you are developing a vision for what you want to do going forward, you must consider two important questions. Is the vision revolutionary, one that involves new ideas for the organization? Or is it evolutionary, one that is new but is essentially the next iteration of an idea or process that already exists within the organization?

As I review my thirty-plus years on Wall Street and replay the thousands of conversations I've had with clients across all industries, internal conversations with teams of which I have been a part as the leader or just as a participant in a conference room discussion, it is clear that very few people have genuinely original thoughts and ideas. I don't mean this to sound arrogant in any way, but as I have listened, *really* listened to some of these discussions, many of the comments made in the room are repeating what has already been said or are questions asking for explanation.

Further, when these new ideas are introduced, if they are truly "out of the box," most participants in the discussion have a very hard time grasping them. Typically, the idea needs to be explained several times. In some cases, it takes several meetings for people to understand it before a decision can be made to move forward. As a result, I have come to the conclusion, as I mentioned in my book *Strategize to Win*, that if you want your organization to embrace and execute a revolutionary vision, you must "educate and sell." You must first develop a narrative to define the idea and explain how it works, what is needed to make it work, and how the outcome or output will impact the organization. Once people understand the idea, then you must sell it in the context of how it will enhance the organization's performance, improve its competitive standing, or create greater value for the shareholders and employees. You must sell, sell, sell from the perspective of every constituent.

If, on the other hand, your vision is evolutionary, then as a leader you must show that the timing is right for an update, a restart, or a makeover. This kind of vision is usually much easier to sell because the organization has already bought into the concept and now needs only to be convinced that the investment in an update will yield a great return.

Selling your vision is one of the most important things you will do in your evolution from individual contributor to leader. If you have been with your organization a long time as an individual contributor, chances are that not many people see you as a potential leader. Your ability to create and sell a vision is one of the most compelling things you can do. That will influence others to recognize your growth and start to consider you as leadership material.

DECISIONS MAKE GOOD LEADERS

The next stop on the leadership journey from individual contributor to leader: Be decisive. A few years back, I had the pleasure of hearing Meg Whitman, then the CEO of eBay, speak at a conference. One of her remarks—"The price of inaction is greater than the cost of making a mistake"—has stuck with me to this day and is a statement especially true for a good leader. You must be decisive; it is a requirement of leadership.

As an individual contributor, your role is to gather data, consult with others, deliberate, study, and ultimately present to decision makers what you have learned. In fact, in many cases, you are rewarded for creating and conducting a thorough process from which others, including you, can make a decision. Your level of success is often tied to the process of gathering this data, not to the final outcome.

However, as you move from individual contributor to leader, your ability to be decisive, your willingness to make the final call, will be a key to your success. You will be evaluated on whether or not you made the right decisions, not on whether you conducted the right research or processes that helped you arrive at the conclusion. As a leader, there will be times when a decision you made goes awry. Others may try to understand how you arrived at your decision, but the focus will be on the decision itself, the one that was ultimately your call.

Being decisive, good or bad, is the hallmark of a great leader. In the military, where there is a clear focus on leadership and creating leaders, soldiers are taught to give orders "in their own name." Even when they are given orders by a general, the colonel does not then say, "The general said . . ." Instead, the colonel gives the order using their own authority and thereby taking responsibility for any action.

When you choose to sit in a leadership seat, you accept the responsibility of making decisions along with the accolades and the penalties and consequences that come with them. During my time on Wall Street, I've seen people in leadership positions make decisions that did not go as expected, and then I watched them immediately look to blame others for the poor outcome. They faulted the vice president for not supervising or checking the associate's work, or the analyst for not verifying the model. They looked to blame anyone but themselves, accepting no responsibility for the failure. This is not an example of poor leadership; it is an example of no leadership. Great leaders own the outcome, whatever it is, even if the information they received led to a fallible decision. A good leader's stance is always "I made the call. It happened on my watch. I am ultimately responsible."

When leaders fail to take responsibility for the outcome, it's not uncommon to see those who report to them lose faith and interest in working for them. When a leader repeatedly blames others for their failures, over time the most talented junior professionals will opt to work on other teams. Eventually, this kind of leader starts having difficulty assembling the best players.

LEADERSHIP GEM:

Poor leadership results in a failure to attract and keep great talent.

Sol was widely known as one of the smartest vice presidents at a large utility. He had risen through the ranks quickly and now had responsibility for managing several teams across three very-high-profile projects that the company was pursuing. There was a tight deadline for a project that had to be blessed by the city council before it could move forward.

The night before the presentation was due to be sent to the council, Sol found a huge error in a calculation, which would result in tens of thousands of dollars being added to the company's proposal. After correcting for this error, the company's proposal might not be competitive enough to win the project. Sol was supposed to have reviewed the numbers a week prior but had failed to do so because he was working on another aspect of the project. When he found the error, he went to the junior manager, who also had a reputation as a superstar within the organization, and went ballistic in front of the other team members. He chewed out the young man literally in front of his peers.

The next day, the presentation did not go well and the utility did not win the business. Sol made a big deal of the loss in the department and told all his superiors about the colossal mistake the young manager had made. Sol never made mention of the fact that he was supposed to have reviewed the work at least a week prior, which would have given the organization time to think of alternative ways to make the bid attractive. The young manager felt that there would be no way to recover from the mistake and left the group a couple of months later. After a few more quarters, he finally left the organization. Sol posted the vacant position internally. But none applied. They were not able to recruit junior professionals from other areas within the organization because Sol had created a reputation for himself as someone who "passed the buck," was not supportive of his team, and had poor oversight on projects. None of the company's other young professionals wanted to work with a manager who would unfairly blame them when things went wrong.

In today's environment, Millennials and Gen Zers care deeply about working for managers who take the time to invest in them. In fact, I would argue that they value personal development more highly than Boomers and Gen Xers have valued it. This is not surprising. Young professionals have access to so many vehicles where they can learn on their own, such as platforms like Google, YouTube, or LinkedIn Learning. Therefore, they *really* value someone who takes the time to teach them something that only experience can teach and they cannot learn on their own.

In addition, because digital communication has made it so easy to share information, people with bad reputations as managers are exposed much faster. If there is a manager or senior leader who is difficult to work with, it takes only one junior professional to send a text or an email to his or her "community" of colleagues. Then everyone on that communication chain would know to avoid working with that person. Twenty years ago, four or five people would have the unfortunate experience of working with a difficult manager before that manager would become the "boss to avoid." In some cases, because Boomers and Gen Xers did not share information in the same way Millennials and Gen Zers do, that reputation might never have been widely shared or solidified. As a result, the difficult manager would have had the opportunity to destroy a lot of great talent. When you consider these facts, it is not hard to understand why industries such as financial services, technology, and industrial engineering were known to have poor reputations for having great managers or training, and why managers who may have been great producers but poor leaders could survive for so long.

DECIDING TO BUILD RELATIONSHIPS

Some of the most successful people, let alone leaders, I know are people who have a myriad of relationships. They understood early in their careers that they did not have to be the smartest people in the room or know everything about a topic. Rather, all they needed to do was to *know* someone who had the right information, had the right answer, or could make something happen.

You've likely heard the phrase "It's not what you know, but who you know." One of the ways people rise throughout organizations is through reputation—who they know and what is said about them. If you, for example, are in a client service or other externally facing role like sales, marketing, finance, or consulting, it is extraordinarily valuable to have someone you are serving talk about how great you are.

Deciding to build and leverage a network is another important step on the path to leadership. No one can succeed alone. Leaders need to leverage other people's intellect, experience, and networks to successfully execute any project or endeavor. We will look more closely at building networks in future chapters, but it is worth noting that as you move from individual contributor to leader, having access to a network of relationships that can support you as you ascend to the leadership seat is critical to your success.

As an individual contributor, you cannot be so focused on your own performance that you fail to build relationships. Throughout my career, I have seen many people advance their career by having clients and other influential people speak highly of them when in conversation with their company's leadership. Each time, this served to move them into a more influential role, enhance their compensation, or advance their career. Nirvana is when this happens organically on its own. But I have also seen people specifically ask their clients or others to "put in a good word for them." I am not going so far as to suggest you follow this strategy. But you do want there to be the possibility it will happen. And failure to develop these networks will handicap your rise, as well as your effectiveness once you get there.

People who are aspiring to be leaders in an organization often look up after a few years of working as an individual contributor and discover they have no network to leverage for access to new opportunities or consideration for leadership roles. They have been so busy processing direct assignments that they failed to understand how their roles fit into the larger organization—or to exhibit curiosity about how it works. While as an individual contributor it is important to show you can do the work, you must simultaneously invest in relationships that are tangential to the job you are currently doing.

LEADERSHIP GEM:

Performance creates the opportunity for mobility within an organization, but it is the relationships that enable and drive mobility.

The more relationships you have across the organization, the more support you will have from various sponsors when your name comes up in closed-door discussions about important leadership roles. In addition, you will be better positioned to have discussions on your own about your aspirations and career trajectory.

Getting involved in enterprise-wide groups and activities, such as recruiting, employee resource groups, volunteer efforts, and cross-divisional projects, is one of the easiest ways to build a network. Doing so often provides opportunities that not only allow you to hone your leadership skills but also offer you the chance to work with people from other areas of the organization and to build relationships.

As a young associate in investment banking, I immersed myself in the company's recruiting effort as soon as I joined the firm's M&A department. This gave me the opportunity to travel to college campuses around the country and interview candidates alongside colleagues who were my peers as well as very senior people from corporate finance, sales and trading, research and capital markets, and other areas.

Working on my projects in M&A, I would often reach out to someone in the research department who could provide me with names of comparable companies, someone from the capital markets team who could help me better understand the trading multiples, or someone from sales and trading who could get me an investor's perspective. Who did I call? The people I'd met when traveling to Cambridge to do recruiting at my alma mater, Harvard undergrad or Business School.

When I later wanted to transition to a role in capital markets, I had access to a network of people who knew me and could help me. As I mentioned earlier, I often recruited alongside senior people as we interviewed and sold candidates on joining the firm. I am sure that some of those senior people contributed to the closed-door discussions about my candidacy for new roles and promotions.

IT'S YOU AND YOUR TEAM

Finally, as an individual contributor, you are primarily serving two constituents: yourself and your team. You are part of a process that produces an outcome and you have a responsibility to your team to do your part to make sure that outcome is a good one. You are serving yourself with your ability to get things done, resulting in a good evaluation, great compensation, promotions, and ultimately success in that role or your career. As a leader, however, it is important to understand that what you do not only impacts your performance, career success, and rise in the organization. It also impacts six other core constituents: (1) your team, the people who execute your vision and bring your plan to fruition; (2) your boss, the person you report to; (3) the organization and all the people who work with your department and therefore touch your seat, who depend on your team's ability to execute and produce; (4) the customers your organization serves; (5) the shareholders who ultimately benefit when your company performs well by producing a profit, increasing its market share, advancing its technology, or outpacing the competition; and (6) the donors who contribute their hard-earned dollars to benefit those served by your organization's philanthropic efforts.

Moving from individual contributor to leader is probably one of the toughest transitions for anyone to make. If you are like most of us, you have been focused on your personal benefit, risks, and potential losses for a number of years. You may or may not even understand the stakes for each of the stakeholders. As you are seeking leadership roles, you must take the time to invest in learning more about each of the constituents and what matters most to each of them, understanding how they would define success for your leadership seat.

For example, your team will care about how you help them develop their skills, how you assign roles and responsibilities, and how you compensate them. They will care about how fair you are as a leader as well as your standing and reputation among other leaders in the organization. Your immediate boss will care about how you execute assignments, make strong decisions, and make your boss look good as the person who hired you. The customers will care if you provide them with the best possible product, and so on. As a leader, it is essential to your success that you remain mindful of these constituents while simultaneously seeking to find outcomes that are the best solution for each. It is not always the case that outcomes will work equally for everyone, but as a leader, your job is to seek to develop outcomes that are as beneficial as possible to all interested parties.

This is one of the reasons you must make sure you are not focused on executing something that someone else on your team could be doing. As a leader your focus must be on problem-solving so that you can come up with the best solution for all your constituents. While as an individual contributor you can afford to be micro-focused on the task at hand, as a leader you must be macro-focused on the bigger picture and how it affects all your constituents.

CHAPTER 2

Knowing How You Want to Lead

LEADERSHIP PEARL #2
*How people feel about you as a leader will impact how
they perform and what they deliver.*

IN GENERAL, THERE are two ways you can ascend to a leadership position in a corporate environment. The first way is to be identified early in your career as someone who has leadership potential. Many organizations call these people high-potential candidates, or "Hi-Pos." These are people who have distinguished themselves by delivering an exceptional work product, demonstrating curiosity about the larger organization, showing an aptitude for building relationships, or showing an appetite and aptitude for leading others.

Generally, human resources (HR) leadership will create programs, roles, and opportunities for this group to help accelerate their development and expose them to the kinds of experiences that will help shape them into leaders within the organization. These programs often offer presentation, organization, management, and even leadership skill building. Hi-Pos are typically first in line to receive assignments that will highlight their talents and give them exposure to the organization's other leaders and decision makers. There will also be difficult and challenging assignments designed to train these prospective leaders on how to make tough decisions, to allocate resources, or simply to build their resilience. HR tracks their progress and development.

Eventually a few of the Hi-Pos are placed on the short list to lead major divisions within the organization or to lead the organization itself. If you are part of this group, usually a sponsor, mentor, or other leader will tell you directly that you are being groomed for a leadership position.

When being groomed for a top role, you will be asked to take on interim positions that will prepare you to lead, manage, or motivate people. These roles are designed to stretch you as a leader. After assuming each job, you must get quickly focused on what type of leader you want to be and how you want to lead. You will want to consider questions such as:

- How do I want to show up as a leader?
- What do I want to do differently than I have done in the previous three years?
- What are the key success factors in this role?
- What are the clear directives that I have from those who put me in this role?
- Who else has this role in the industry whom I might be able to speak to?
- What three words do I want senior staff or the board of directors to use when describing me?
- What words do I want former peers to use to describe me?
- How do I want junior staff to describe me, experience me?
- What are the organization's other important imperatives in addition to maximizing profits?
- What gaps do I see in the organization that I can use this role to fill?
- Is there a challenge or crisis for me to solve?

- If I were going to be in this role for only three years, what would I want to have accomplished?
- Who do I want in my innermost circle?
- Who will be my external advisors?
- Whom do I trust to tell me the truth about the real information I need from various parts of the organization to make the right decisions on behalf of all the stakeholders?

This last question is particularly important to consider. When you get to a leadership seat, it is more difficult to get honest information from those around you. There are very few people who are willing to tell the boss the real, unadulterated truth. Most of the time, people assume that the boss does not want to hear bad news or what you *really think* about an issue, especially if their view is different from yours. While there are some leaders who want to surround themselves with "yes" people who will always agree with them, great leaders want people around them who will give their honest opinions and are not afraid to speak truth to power. They understand that the way to lead in a manner that is best for the organization is to make decisions with complete, factual information or to gain perspectives from people they trust to give them their honest view.

LEADERSHIP GEM:

Great leaders surround themselves with people who will tell them the truth. The ability to speak the truth as well as hear it is a key attribute of great leadership.

When you get to the leadership seat, you must present yourself as someone who wants to hear the truth and what people really think. You make it clear that you are not going to "shoot the messenger." If people feel that it will be an unpleasant experience to give you facts or real opinions, they just won't do it. If this happens, your problem is that you cannot fix what you don't know is broken.

I was once in an intimate fireside chat event with a CEO I greatly admire. During the Q&A, an audience member asked him, "How do you know at your level that you are getting the right information?" His answer was very insightful. "There are two ways that you can get the information you need to effectively run your organization," he said. "First, you can surround yourself with very good leaders who report to you and on whom you can rely for information about their respective businesses. However, if you do that, you had better be absolutely sure that they are telling you the truth, not just their version of it. Understand, however, that you are completely vulnerable to them and how they handle information."

He went on further to say, "Secondly, you can take the extra time to get to know people throughout your organization. Build relationships with the security guard, the cleaning lady, the first-year associates, vice presidents on up to people who are executive vice presidents. Spend time with them so they feel that they can trust you and that you see them, and they will give you information and/or corroborate or refute information that you ask them about. They will provide you with the data that will give you confidence about what your direct reports are telling you, or cause you to ask more probing questions until you get to the truth. I am a leader who engages with the second strategy, and it has led me to render very good decisions for the people in my organization."

As you sit in a leadership seat, you will learn that people talk to you in a different way than they did when you were an individual contributor. Both the topics and the delivery change. You are not apt to even get the same kind of information you easily received on your journey to leadership. Since you are now in a position of greater power, you also carry the potential to inspire more fear. It is important that you have a way of accessing information that will give you a sense of what your people really want and how they really feel. This will enable you to make decisions that result in a positive difference for those with whom you work. Do not allow yourself to get isolated from your people, particularly not in this environment where Millennials and Gen Zers have become a major segment of the workforce. These generations highly value engagement and community, particularly in the workplace.

But what if your rise to a leadership position is the result of a complete surprise? You are going along in your career and functioning as a great number two or three to the top person. Then suddenly, someone leaves or there is some kind of crisis or leadership shake-up, and without warning and frankly no training, you are thrust into a leadership position . . . you are IT!

Throughout my career, I have studied various leaders across industries, and I've concluded that there is a direct correlation between organizational crises and women and people of color being named to top leadership roles. Consider companies like Time Warner, HP, GM, American Express, Citibank, Merck, and McDonald's, and even the United States' and the State of New York's governments. In each case, they were at a critical crisis point when the nod was given to a woman or person of color.

The lesson? If you are a woman or a person of color in a senior position, I encourage you to be particularly intentional about preparing yourself to lead. Your chance to do so could very well come unexpectedly because of some major change or upheaval . . . during the next crisis!

LEADERSHIP GEM:

When the opportunity to lead presents itself, it's too late to start to prepare. Whether it's taking leadership classes, taking on stretch assignments or projects, or reading books like this one, do what you need to be ready when the door opens.

IF IT HAPPENS TO YOU, WHAT DO YOU DO?

After you decide to take on the position, first assess the current environment and determine the organization's, department's, or team's immediate and intermediate needs. Next, you must then intentionally think about *how* you want to lead.

How do you want people to see you as a leader? If you have been named the CEO, for example, how do you want to be perceived by your board of directors, your direct leadership team, your former peers, your employees, and external constituents (shareholders, customers, competitors, etc.)? One of the most important things to remember is that you are not just the CEO for a particular team or division but rather for the entire company, with all its diverse businesses, internal and external stakeholders, and, if it is a public company, its shareholders.

As a CEO, your direct bosses are the board of directors, represented in most cases by the chair of the board. Make no mistake, the board's job is to represent and protect the shareholders' best interests. You want them to conclude that they have made the right choice as soon as possible after you have taken on the CEO role. You want the board to see you as someone who respects others' opinions, as collaborative, strategic, decisive, and driven by the organization's best interests versus your own. Remember, especially if this is a surprise appointment, you will inherit the board and your direct reports, and therefore you won't likely have had much one-on-one interaction with the board members. Therefore, it will be important for you to be intentional about getting to know them individually by spending time with them as soon as possible.

One of my close friends, a senior executive at a Fortune 250 company, used a very effective tool for swiftly and efficiently building relationships with key constituents, including board members. She would schedule a forty-five-minute face-to-face meeting, with one agenda item designed to get an understanding of who that person was. She would ask them to tell her their life story and philosophy, what drove them, how they made decisions, what was most important to them about working with other people, etc. At the end, she would ask for another forty-five-minute meeting. At the next meeting, she would spend about twenty minutes sharing her life story, emphasizing some of her tough personal experiences and how they spurred the most personal growth. She would then use the remaining twenty-five minutes of the meeting to share her view of the company's most urgent imperatives and to solicit the board member's feedback. During the conversation, she would intentionally use words and examples that painted a clear picture of her as collaborative, decisive, empathetic, and strategic. Because she had established a personal connection at those previous meetings, when she later had to interact with each person in a board context, she already had a good sense of the many personalities around the table, and they had a perception of her that had been influenced by their previous conversations. From the start, this allowed her to begin building relationships from a constructive perspective as well as from the established perception that she wanted them to have of her.

As I discussed in my book *Expect to Win*, the way you train people to think about you is to execute behavior that is consistent with the adjectives you want people to use to describe you when you are not in the room. As a leader, at a minimum you want the board to say that you are thoughtful, strategic, a great executor, and a great relationship builder, which means that everything you do should in some way demonstrate each one of these attributes. When you are speaking to members of the board, you want to be mindful to also use these words when you are describing yourself as they get to know you.

LEADING YOUR DIRECT REPORTS

As you begin in your new role as the head of your team, it will be important to quickly establish yourself as a collaborative leader. Your success will be highly dependent on your ability to elicit the absolute best output each team member has to offer. It will be important for you to be respectful and, in some cases, even deferential toward their experience and expertise. You could potentially inherit a leadership team that has more years of experience than you. Like you, some of them may have even been considered for the top job that you won. If that is the case, you will want to meet with them individually, as soon as possible, to understand whether they are willing and able to continue giving their very best under your leadership. If not, you will have to choose a successor for their role, thoughtfully and quickly.

One of the most important first steps that you can take—after settling the crisis, of course—is to go on a listening tour. This will help you understand the people in your organization—what is on their minds, how they feel about how things have been going, where the gaps are, what could be done better, and what is working just fine. In your first few interactions with your new team, be inclusive and collaborative, intentionally soliciting everyone's voice and opinion on matters big and small. After you have had a chance to have several meetings and understand the most urgent issues the organization is facing, then you must quickly establish priorities and your expectations of each member of your team. Immediately working to empower this team very early in your tenure as CEO or leader will serve you well as you move swiftly to establish and execute the company's future goals.

LEADERSHIP GEM:

The best leaders are active listeners.

Even if you are a leader of a private company or nonprofit, you will still likely have a board of directors to answer to. However, in this case, they will be more focused on what is best for the company, particularly over the longer term, and less on quarterly performance, including Wall Street's earnings expectations and the negative consequences on stock price should the company perform below those expectations.

As a leader in a private context, you want to make sure that your board sees you as someone who is a strategic thinker and an executor. If you are in an industry where compensation is historically lower than in many other industries, then you want to be seen as a great relationship builder. You will be more likely to keep great talent because they like working for your organization, its leadership, the demeanor of their peers, access to large developmental opportunities, or a sense of belonging—each largely being driven by YOU!

While I have clearly focused on leadership at the very top to this point, my advice is no different if you are a leader at other levels within your organization or company. Your stakeholders will have very similar expectations around your ability to collaborate, build teams, motivate and inspire people, think strategically, and execute a plan. The primary difference is that while you want to be seen in this way, you also want to know and understand as well as exhibit some of the qualities common to the organization's more senior leaders so that people start to "see" you in those more senior roles.

I like to say that those under your leadership "experience you" or "consume you." They walk away from interacting with you with a feeling about you and about themselves, and you have the power to influence that feeling. Do you want them to walk away feeling inspired, encouraged, or happy that they are working with and for you? Or do you want them to walk away feeling afraid, discouraged, demotivated, or wishing they were working with or for someone else? It's your decision. And keep in mind . . . how someone feels about you as a leader will impact how they perform and what they deliver.

Because most people fail to consider how THEY want to lead or who they want to be as a leader, and how they want to train for that, they lead others in the same way they were led. In addition, while many industries and companies train people how to do a certain job, they rarely intentionally teach them how to lead, motivate, or inspire other people. There are a few exceptions, however, such as GE, GM, Chrysler, and Exxon, where there are very well-developed, long-term training programs where leaders are rotated in the organization to learn the business and also to have an opportunity to lead in different situations as well as to observe other leaders.

Many of these companies have reputations for creating great leaders. In the 1980s, 1990s, and even into the first few years of the millennium, GE was widely known for its leadership training. By the time a professional arrived at running one of GE's top businesses, or was in a C-suite role, they were deemed ready to run the company. Earning a top position at GE meant that you were virtually in line to succeed Jack Welch, the then CEO who orchestrated many successive quarters of outstanding performance for the company, driving the stock price to some of its highest levels in the company's history. If someone was trained and ascended to a position reporting directly to Jack Welch, but it became clear that they did not have what it took to lead at GE, many of them left or went on to become CEOs of other Fortune 500 companies.

When people who have not been trained or did not intentionally prepare themselves to lead are thrust into a leadership seat, they do what comes naturally to them, typically behaving as they have seen other leaders do. Unfortunately, this often perpetuates bad leadership behavior. I saw this phenomenon in investment banking during the eighties and nineties. During this period, Wall Street was known as a "rough and tough" environment with a poor reputation for managing people. It was widely known that the way to get to the most senior position of managing director was to be an outstanding producer—the banker or trader with the most revenues listed next to their name. In producer cultures like Wall Street, people are rewarded not only with outsize compensation, promotions, and titles but often with management and leadership positions, with little regard for their ability to be a great leader who can motivate, teach, and inspire others. It was not at all uncommon for someone who was, for example, an M&A banker and a top revenue producer, or a top salesman or trader, to be named to lead a group, department, or division. These people were rarely trained to lead yet ascended to a leadership seat. However, their subsequent behavior was such that their reports did not work for them very long. Their departments typically experienced very high turnover during their tenure, yet these managers remained in their roles because they were outstanding producers, often contributing outsize revenue to their organizations.

Terry worked for Mike, the head of the department. Mike had a reputation for being very gruff and short, often openly expressing his displeasure and "chewing out" the people who worked for him on the trading floor in front of their colleagues. In fact, when someone or something upset him, he was known for slamming down and breaking the phones attached to the turrets on trading floors. Terry was one of the few people on the trading floor who could work for Mike, often accommodating and supporting his behavior with some displays of his own toughness.

In his own circles with his peers and even with the people he managed, Terry was known as a reasonable guy who was fair and listened to his people. One day, the group was called together by Mike's boss and told that Mike was no longer at the firm and Terry would take on the role of leading and managing the department. Terry had learned about the change only a couple of hours before the rest of the group when he was asked to take on the role, to which he agreed. In his first team meeting, Terry told the group it would be business as usual, and everyone was expected to "continue to do their jobs the way they always had."

Terry managed the team in the same way Mike had, including berating people, publicly displaying displeasure, even banging a phone or two on the desk. One by one, the team's other star players, formerly Terry's peers, started to leave both the team and the firm. To replace them, Terry had to recruit from outside the firm. While these recruits were excited about the new opportunity, they didn't know the firm or the clients. Terry had to let them get settled in, in some cases be trained, and learn how to assimilate and work with the incumbent team. As a result, the group's profitability suffered, and they started to lose market share in the industry.

Unfortunately, Terry's success as a leader was negatively impacted. Instead of trusting his own instincts about how to lead and motivate people, he thought the best way to lead was to imitate Mike, his former boss. After all, the organization had rewarded and promoted Mike. What Terry did not know, however, was that Mike was asked to leave the company because the organization had started to notice how many strong, talented professionals were leaving as a result of Mike's poor leadership. Terry also failed to consider all the things he had heard as a member of Mike's team, the things his peers disliked about Mike's leadership, and all the things that he himself did not like about Mike's leadership. Terry never asked himself, "If Mike could be successful leading the way he did, how much more could I accomplish if I led in a way that inspired the team and made them excited to work for me and to be a part of my success?"

Many organizations have traditionally rewarded people like Mike because they were great producers. Interestingly, at the same time, these organizations would verbally praise people known to be excellent at developing young professionals and retaining strong talent, but they would not reward them in the same way they did producers like Mike. In today's war for talent, organizations must show they truly value people who can attract, develop, and retain great talent as much as they value producers who do an outstanding job generating revenue. The reality is, in most organizations people generate the behavior that is rewarded. If someone is showing behavior that is unbecoming of a leader but is still clearly rewarded with promotions or outsize pay, then it sends a strong message to the rest of the organization that this behavior is not only tolerated, but valued.

I often marvel at how people change when they are offered the privilege of leading others. I've seen previously great team members, once critical of overbearing, unsupportive leaders blinded by their own biases and ways of thinking, become exactly that when they stepped into the top spot. Apparently, people think it's easier to do what seems to work for other people rather than developing their own style of leadership that is true to who they are. Authenticity, of course, by definition, would be more effective and inspirational. Ironically, following someone else's leadership template, especially when it's "my way or the highway," the norm for decades, does little to inspire or drive innovation.

When your team is confined by your "my way" leadership rather than being motivated and inspired by you, they will fear you, which only further constrains their productivity. If your team sees you as intolerant of new ideas and ways of thinking, as someone who must do everything your way, it will curb their creativity and productivity. They will fail to venture outside your direction, and you will be robbed of the opportunities to lead your team to outsize success. Why? Because your team members' contributions will result from *your* thinking and limitations rather than from who they are, *their* ideas, intellect, experiences, and creativity, which, frankly, could all be far beyond yours.

Bill led a team at an advertising firm. He believed he was chosen for the role because he was the smartest guy among his peers. The firm was tasked with expanding the consumer brand of a new version of a soft drink. The brand executives were particularly keen to reach consumers where they previously had very little penetration: multicultural and female consumers. Bill's team members Tess and Phyllis had come from these communities and had very solid ideas about what they believed would be an effective campaign. However, these ideas were the opposite of Bill's. Both Tess and Phyllis were hesitant to offer their suggestions. A few months back, they had witnessed another colleague challenge Bill's ideas, and his reactions were swift, harsh, and public. As a result, that colleague became demoralized and quiet, rarely speaking up or sharing ideas or information with the group.

Bill called the team together and put forth an idea for the soft-drink commercial. While he asked for the group's input, he did so in a way that effectively took away his team's voice. "Our executives are asking whether this commercial could be construed as offensive by multicultural consumers," Bill said. "I think that it is nonsense, and we should move forward as planned. What do you all think?"

Given the dynamics of Bill's leadership style and his history of displeasure when someone challenged him, no one in the group dared to speak. Tess finally offered, "Well, I think the message in the commercial plays on a stereotype of that group as being very aggressive and it might be poorly received and taken the wrong way. I think that we have to be careful about taking that group's loyalty for granted."

Bill swiftly responded, "I think you are being too sensitive; no one will think that way. They will love it. We are going to recommend this to the client. You should think about things before you say them."

There were other team members who agreed with Tess, but no one dared say a word, particularly after Bill's response to Tess. Bill and his team recommended the commercial to the client, who produced it and put it on the air. The commercial was very poorly received. The social media response, particularly from the very consumer group the client wanted to attract, was harsh and negative. The public backlash lasted for weeks. Not only was the new product denounced, but a few consumers started a negative campaign aimed at the company's other products. As a result, the company lost market share in its category to its competitors. After several weeks, the company pulled the commercial off the air. Needless to say, Bill's firm was not asked to submit a proposal for the company's next brand launch, and Bill was subsequently reassigned to a new role, which effectively took him off the track for promotion to a more senior role.

When you take on a leadership role, I urge you to ask yourself, "How do I want people to experience me, to consume me, as a leader?" Think of the leaders who have inspired you either positively or negatively. Think of the people you have admired or been excited to work for or even wished you could have worked for. As you look back on your career, who are the leaders you've interacted with or observed who taught you something valuable, or for whom you would gladly work today? And conversely, who would you rather quit than have to work for again?

LEADERSHIP GEM:

While how you see yourself is important, how others see you is critical to your success as a leader.

As I developed my own leadership style, this was a very useful exercise for me. I've reported to a few leaders for whom, even at this stage of my career, I would work for anywhere, anytime. When I did this exercise, I thought of leaders who took the time to teach me the critical things I needed to consider when thinking about a transaction; those who showed me how to speak to investors and the salespeople representing the investors; and those who taught me valuable deal terminology. I thought about the senior associates and young vice presidents working in M&A when I first started my career, who guided me on how to construct models or do comparable company analysis when the person leading my transaction failed to teach me how to do so.

In addition, when doing this exercise, I also considered leaders with poor reputations as deal captains; leaders of whom people were terrified; and leaders who were not supportive of their team and who, when something went wrong, would blame their own team members before considering that members of other departments could be at fault. I learned as much from these poor leaders as I did from great ones about how NOT to behave as a leader. When I had the privilege of leading a group of people, I wanted them to consume me in a positive way. In fact, I developed a vision for myself as a leader, as someone who was seen as supportive, encouraging, motivating, collaborative, respectful, inspiring, and honest. I wanted the people who worked for me to feel protected, to know I always had their backs. Then, I set out to behave that way.

As you think about how you want to be consumed as a leader, you must also consider the context or environment in which you are leading and if it will tolerate different styles of leadership. In the eighties and nineties, one of the constraints of leading in the financial services industry was that there seemed to be one dominant style of leadership. As I've noted, the "my way" style dominated most investment banks and was rewarded over other approaches. While each bank had its own culture, when you surveyed most successful traders, bankers, and even leaders at the top of the house, they all demonstrated some version of this type of leadership.

Interestingly enough, it was also an industry characterized by a large number of "characters" or "difficult personalities." It experienced a high rate of employee burnout, failed first marriages, and other by-products of working with tough, difficult leaders. While the industry certainly generated a lot of revenue over those two decades, I often wondered how much more could have been generated if the younger professionals, in particular, felt valued and were inspired by their leaders. Would they have been better positioned to invest their very best at those companies?

If you work in an industry or company known for leaders with one type of leadership profile, it might be difficult to show up and be successful using a different style. I've given several talks on leadership at technology firms and have been advised by the seminar organizers that their culture was dominated by engineers. Typically, their style tends to be very black and white, lacking collaboration, and showing little respect for people who are not engineers, thereby making the culture very difficult for people with other backgrounds. Yet, even in these environments, to be innovative and create products that are attractive to many different consumers, these organizations need to attract employees with diverse backgrounds and expertise.

While it may be challenging to show up and use a different leadership style than the prevailing one in that culture, if the company hired you, then perhaps one of the things they valued about you is that very ability to lead differently. Before you fall in line with the pack, if you know you have been successful in generating great productivity from your teams in the past, then follow the script that has worked for you before, even if you tailor it slightly to fit in the box of the new culture.

If you are a leader who developed your career in a similar environment but developed a different leadership style, it is likely you have developed enough of a reputation and strong relationships to be able to introduce an alternative way to lead and find a way to success.

If you joined the organization and were laterally recruited, it could be more difficult to be successful in such a dominant culture. To do so, you should focus on spending time with middle-level managers and junior employees to build relationships and better understand who they are, how they learn, what motivates and inspires them, and how to get the highest level of productivity from them. The time you spend with this group should be disproportionately more than with your peers. As you establish your own style, this group will support and help you establish yourself as a leader.

We are fortunate to be at a time in history when corporate cultures are being tested and redefined. We have all lived through the changes and crises of 2020—the COVID-19 global pandemic; social unrest resulting from centuries of racial inequities in the United States; worldwide immigrant needs and governmental leadership changes; the emergence of social media as a powerful democratizing tool; and the emergence of Millennials and Gen Zers as the dominant populations in the workforce. Corporate leaders are realizing that a new leadership paradigm is required. They recognize the need to be more authentic, show more empathy, and think about transparency as one of the table stakes in leading.

LEADERSHIP GEM:

Today's employees are looking for authenticity. No other leader is exactly like you; your distinguishing characteristic and sharing who you really are will build connection with your employees.

In the last year, I have had many conversations with leaders at various levels and it is clear that many of them have never brought their true, authentic selves to the seats of power they hold today. In the past, they chose consciously or unconsciously to assimilate into corporate cultures, adjusting who they were to be successful. This was quite easy to do since most corporate cultures across most industries were clearly defined with a predominant and well-known way to get ahead. As a result, leaders knew what they had to do to be successful. If that meant checking the real you at the door, then so be it.

Over time, however, there were problems with this approach. If you were not mindful, or self-aware, you lost yourself, evolving into someone else, losing touch with your authenticity and ability to integrate who you were into the organization's culture. This reality has created a dilemma for many leaders today. Their employees are demanding a level of engagement, transparency, empathy, and vulnerability that is foreign to and, in fact, quite difficult for many leaders. If this describes you, it is time for you to give serious thought to the essence of this chapter and define how you can be received as an authentic leader. It will be critical to your current and future ability to attract and motivate the right team and lead them to success.

CHAPTER 3

Knowing How to Assess Talent: Choosing and Motivating the Right Team

LEADERSHIP PEARL #3
Choosing the right team will define your legacy.

Two of the most important things you will ever do as a leader are to choose and to motivate your team. If you work for a large organization with a well-oiled human resources (HR) division, you will have access to resources that will help you source, evaluate, and onboard candidates. Experienced people will help you conduct interviews and choose the talent that is right for your team and will also easily fit into the company culture.

But for those who own their own businesses, the story is different. If you are an entrepreneur and leader of your own high-growth organization, you likely have far fewer resources at your disposal or experience to help you hire effectively.

LEADING IN A COMPANY YOU STARTED

As an entrepreneur, you will have the opportunity to build your team from scratch. Your company is in its early days and growing quickly, so you may not feel that you have the luxury of spending much time focusing on building a team. You need bodies who can execute, and you need them fast.

However, it is important to take the time to assess who you are bringing into your company, especially in the early stages of growth. A wrong hire, particularly at the senior level, can be very expensive from a compensation or ownership standpoint, as well as detrimental to the fledgling culture you are trying to build. In fact, a bad hire can literally ruin a new company. It is important to carefully assess the company's needs and have a process to assess the potential hire's skill set so you can be clear on how they can fulfill those needs. The mistake I see many early-stage CEOs make is hiring someone like themselves instead of someone who fills a leadership gap and brings different skills and abilities to the table.

If you have not had a lot of experience interviewing candidates, consider assembling a "kitchen cabinet"—a group of professionals who have experience hiring people, have worked as HR professionals, or have expertise in the specific roles you are hiring for. They can help you choose the right candidates. Many early-stage CEOs mistakenly make critical hiring decisions without the benefit of experienced interviewers, only to regret those decisions later. They end up losing valuable time executing company strategy, instead investing inordinate amounts of time trying to repair and rebuild their company's culture after a hiring mistake.

Get your kitchen cabinet to help you think through the job description and what you really need from a potential hire. Then conduct the initial interviews and pass the candidates through to this small group to interview as well. The group can assess and advise you on what they learned. Based on this additional information, you can make the final decision about how to fill the role. If you have no real experience hiring people, you may even want to have your kitchen cabinet do the first few rounds of interviews for you, using the criteria that you've established together with them. This will help narrow down the list. Then you can prepare to do the last round of interviews yourself, using the original criteria but also assessing whether or not YOU can work with this person.

Now, if you are an entrepreneur with fewer than five years of experience, have no interviewing skills, or do not have a network of people you can rely on to find candidates, then you may find it difficult to add people to your team. You might not know what a senior sales leader is supposed to do or what the critical tasks of a chief financial officer or a treasurer are. Further, you may not have a real sense of how to tell if a person can do the job you are hiring them for. Please do not fall prey to the temptation to just jump in, start interviewing, and then hire someone. You will put yourself in the position to be taken advantage of by someone who may be more experienced than you or who is an extremely smooth talker or impressive interviewer. If the person cannot deliver, it could not only cause harm to your company but also compromise other people's confidence in you as a leader.

LEADERSHIP GEM:

As an entrepreneurial leader, you cannot do it all. Building yourself a "kitchen cabinet" or group of supporters who offer the skills you don't have is the key to your success.

If you lack experience interviewing people, you can go online to find general job descriptions of key roles like CFO, COO, CAO, senior sales officer, chief marketing officer, etc. You can then ask people in your entrepreneurial network, or entrepreneurs who have participated in business accelerators, for the job descriptions they have used. You can also use your academic network. For example, if you graduated from an MBA program, you can ask some of your former professors of marketing, finance, operations, and the like what they look for in a top professional in each of those disciplines. You can also look at the backgrounds of people who are working in these jobs at your competitors to assess if you should further refine your own criteria. If you are a venture-backed company, the partners in the venture capital firm that invested in you can give you names of potential candidates. They have exposure to many companies and generally note the good talent they spot in the companies they meet, even if they do not ultimately invest in them. These venture capitalists also have extensive corporate networks that they can access on your behalf. Once you have a general idea of the functions of these key roles, you can add specifics that might be particular to your company's needs or culture.

Another alternative is to enlist the help of an executive recruiter. While there are large established executive recruiting firms that specialize in recruiting candidates for C-suite roles—chief executive officer (CEO), chief financial officer (CFO), chief marketing officer (CMO), chief administrative officer (CAO), chief operating officer (COO), chief diversity officer (CDO), chief technology officer (CTO), chief investment officer (CIO), chief human resources officer (CHRO)—increasingly, there are executive recruiting firms that were formed specifically to serve the needs of senior officers in early-stage companies. These firms can help you find candidates who have experience working not only for large corporations but also in earlier-stage companies, where the demands are different from those of large, established corporations.

These firms can also be helpful in consulting with you on compensation packages that would be attractive to such candidates. As an early-stage company CEO, you may not be in the position to offer the cash compensation that a large corporation could offer, and you do not want to offer too much of your company's stock to someone who may not work out over the long term as your company grows and its value increases.

If you find yourself in the position where you do not have the resources to engage an executive recruiter or you do not have the relationships to assemble a kitchen cabinet, don't despair. Here are a few questions you might ask in interviews to help you to discern whether the candidates are the right talent for you. I also offer you the rationale for the question and what you might learn.

General Questions to Ask

1. Tell me about yourself.

Rationale: This question will give you a general idea about the person. You will learn a lot by where they choose to start the story. In general, a great candidate should use this question to give you not only a sense of where they are from but also what motivates them, why they have made some of their important decisions, i.e., why they chose the schools they attended, why they took on certain jobs, key decision points in their career, and why they are interested in the role you are offering. If a candidate fails to tell the story with an emphasis on the things that would make them attractive for this job, that is usually a red flag for me.

2. What interests you in this role?

Rationale: A candidate's answer to this question is an important one. As the leader who is hiring this person, you want to be clear that the person has done their homework on your company and on the role of the open position, and has a cogent argument as to why it makes sense for them and what they can contribute. Beware: If a candidate says to you that they are looking for a change but cannot give you a good reason why this role and YOUR company makes sense for them and YOU, this is not the right talent for you; do not hire this person. They may very well be running from another job situation, and you do not want your company to be their first stop. They have probably not thought through what makes sense for them and might quickly become disillusioned with the role and your company. I caution you against hiring someone who is not sure of what they want. Nor do you want to be in the position of spending too much time trying to sell the job to a potential candidate. That is time you cannot afford, given the likely pace of growth of your company and the urgency of your need for talent. While you will have to do *some* selling in an interview, which is perfectly normal for any employer, having to work to convince someone to take on a role could be a signal that it is not the right fit for them or you.

3. **What do you see as three of the most important success factors for this role?**

Rationale: The answers to this question will help you to understand whether the person really knows what it takes to do the job. They will most likely give you reasons why they chose these success factors and add a few more that they believe will be important. You should match up these answers with the job description that you developed with your key advisors. There are general things you need to look for in certain roles. For example, if you are hiring someone for the CFO role, you must know if they have ever been a CFO before, if they have experience accounting for options, if they have ever been involved in fundraising or a public company offering. If you are hiring for a CMO, you want to know what products they have marketed before, the level of their social media skills, and their understanding of basic Google analytics, for example. If you are hiring a chief sales or revenue officer, you want to know their sales targets from their last role, how they were compensated, how they drove sales, or how they identified customer targets.

4. **What do you need in this role to be successful?**

Rationale: In this question, you want to discern if the person is self-motivated, is resourceful, and, frankly, has the scrappiness to be successful in a start-up or early-stage company environment, or rather, if they would need a lot of the resources that are found only in large corporations. More important, you want to understand if the person is going to be highly reliant on you to give them direction and feedback to do the job. In the early days of any job, everyone needs feedback to make sure their actions are aligned with their leader's expectations. But in a fast-paced, high-growth, or crisis-driven environment, you cannot afford to hand-hold one of your senior executives.

5. What motivates you?

Rationale: The candidate's answer to this question will tell you a lot about what inspires the candidate and keeps them going. You are trying to get at what makes them happy and inspires them to really deliver. If you are hiring for a CHRO role, you want to hear an answer like "I am motivated by seeing people succeed or finding out how to unlock the best in the talent that I hire." Or "I am motivated by trying to solve the problems that stop people from delivering their best or creating programs that create greater employee engagement." In some way the answer needs to be about people and people-related issues.

6. What kind of leader motivates you? Can you describe the kind of leader that would motivate you to deliver your very best work?

Rationale: While many of us are self-motivated and can generally inspire ourselves to achieve goals, there is no question that as humans, we are encouraged, stimulated, and motivated by other people, especially great leaders. However, the converse is also true. Most of us are demotivated and sometimes even paralyzed by poor leaders or people who just don't align with our values. The candidate's answer to this question is extremely important because if they describe someone who is the exact opposite of you, that tells you there might not be alignment between you and the candidate.

7. How would you describe yourself as a leader?

Rationale: I frankly love to ask this question of senior leaders I am hiring. It tells me not only what they think of themselves but also how thoughtful they are as leaders about how others might consume them. It also gives me a sense of whether they understand their level of responsibility for developing, motivating, teaching, and inspiring those who work with them. I understand from their answer to this question whether our values as leaders are aligned. It allows me to understand whether they might fit into the vision I have for the culture I am trying to create, or in your case as an entrepreneur, the vision you have for the culture of your company. You will also be able to tell whether this person will have the ability to identify great talent and build teams. Remember that, as the CEO, you won't be able to identify, interview, and bring on every member of your company as it scales and grows; it is just not efficient. You, therefore, will have to rely on others to build their teams and motivate and inspire them to make outsize contributions, which is partly why you are hiring them as a senior member of your team.

I know of one early-stage company CEO who insisted on approving every résumé and seeing every candidate as he built his company. By the time he had almost two thousand employees, the process had become untenable. The senior HR people he hired—each very, very skilled at recruiting and hiring talent—were starting to feel compromised and demotivated. They felt that the CEO didn't trust them to make good decisions, and they were starting to look for jobs outside the company. The CEO was starting to feel frustrated because he could not keep up with the number of candidates, given the organization's need for talent as they experienced hypergrowth.

He was afraid to let go of the process because he thought he would lose the essence of the company culture that existed when he had only two hundred employees. The company continued to be successful, and the CEO finally relinquished his control over the hiring process, allowing the experts that HE had hired to do the jobs he hired them to do. The company experienced a very successful public market exit, through an initial public offering (IPO). But the question remains: How much faster might the company have grown if the CEO had empowered the senior people he so carefully hired to perpetuate the culture by using their expertise to hire the people needed to support growth?

If you are careful and discerning at the onset as you build your senior team, you will no doubt be successful in choosing people who have the right skills to do the job, share your values, and buy into your vision of the company's present and future culture. If your people do not feel that you trust them, then they will become suspicious and begin not to trust you. Empower and trust them to do the job you hired them to do. In essence, TRUST YOURSELF as the leader until otherwise notified!

8. Give me two examples of times that you have failed, when things did not go well.

Rationale: As an early-stage company CEO, you want to hire a senior-level candidate who is resilient and has had some experience with failure. As we all have learned, the more experience you have with failure, the more resilient you become. When you successfully handle failure and convert the experience into valuable lessons, you have more tools for subsequent attempts. In the early days of any company's development, there will be many times when you fail. For example, the fundraising process may go more slowly than anticipated, you may have to lay off staff, the customer converts may not materialize, and so on. The people you add to your senior team need to be able to push through those failures and disappointments. You want to hire someone who is solution oriented and excited about developing a plan B, C, or D if need be, and you want evidence of their ability to do so, which is why this question is so very important.

9. Give me a sense of the key deliverables in your last role.

Rationale: This is an important question because you do not want to take for granted that just because a candidate's last role had a senior title that they had critical deliverables for which they were DIRECTLY responsible. Within their answer to this question, you will also learn something about their judgment and what they define as key or critical to the organization. Listen closely to the answer to this question and probe as much as you need to. You should also compare what they delivered before to what YOU are expecting them to deliver.

10. What impact do you believe you had in your last organization?

Rationale: This question will elicit data that you can use to compare in your due diligence reference calls about the candidate. You will want to compare the impact that he or she says they had with what the previous employers say about what they contributed. You should also try to understand the impact that was expected of them in the role they had, and what they contributed, without being asked, that was valuable.

11. Would your last or current employer agree with the impact you had, or what might they say differently?

Rationale: This question will give you insight into how the candidate thought and felt about the last place they worked or are currently working. Another question you might use in its place is "Tell me about your current or last place of employment." However, most candidates know they should not disparage their last or current employer, and this question is obviously asking for that feedback. If you use the language suggested above, it is trying to elicit the same information but in a way that might produce the data you are looking for.

12. If you were to receive an offer for this role, what would be your thirty-day plan to show that you were a great hire?

Rationale: The candidate's answer to this question will tell you about a few important things, such as how much research they have done on the role, their relative understanding of the challenges and opportunities, how much they have thought about ways to be productive and successful in the role, whether they are prepared for it, and their orientation toward delivering results.

13. What are your two biggest strengths and the one thing that you know you need to continue to work on?

Rationale: This is one of the traditional questions that have been used in interviews for decades. Many companies find other ways to ask this question because it has been so overused. I, however, still like asking this question in this way because it is straightforward, and I am always interested to hear how candidates think of themselves and what they consider to be their strongest assets. It is also interesting to note whether the strengths line up with the key success factors of the job or whether they say that the one thing they need to work on is something I consider to be a necessary skill for the job.

14. I have a panel of people to whom I present candidates. What is the argument you want me to deliver as to why I should hire you for this role?

Rationale: This question gives the candidate one more opportunity to sell themself. If a candidate can deliver a narrative that makes a compelling case that they understand the needs of the position and the needs of the company, and that they have the background and experience to deliver the results you need, then they should at least make the short list of final candidates or get the job, assuming all their references check out.

15. **If you are considering a candidate who has worked only in large corporations, ask these questions: What makes you believe you will be able to work in a start-up? What do you believe are the fundamental differences between large corporations and start-ups? Have you ever worked without an administrative assistant?**

Rationale: These are critical questions for you as an early-stage CEO. Many outstanding candidates who have terrific experience and skills but have worked only in a large corporate setting are used to the tremendous resources available in such an environment. When these candidates transition to a start-up where there is a small group of people, there are no real teams, and everyone is expected to pitch in to do everything, they often have an extremely hard time adjusting. These scenarios often don't work out because the new hire is not used to an environment that does not provide the "comforts" of big corporations, such as having an assistant, someone to answer phones, make travel arrangements, and keep them stocked with pens, paper, and paper clips.

After You Hire

If you are sitting on the other side of the desk during this interview and have never managed a group of people before, one of the most important things you can do is to be clear in your direction of what you want done. If you are unsure of what you need, then invite the team to collaborate and brainstorm with you. The worst thing you can do as a leader is to fail to admit when you are not sure about something and send the team off on a series of wild goose chases as you change your mind over and over. The team will quickly become unmotivated and disillusioned and start to look elsewhere for opportunities.

In this case, you might want to say something like "I am not sure of how we might accomplish this, so I could use the benefit of your intellect and experience. Here is where I would like us to go. Are there any thoughts about how we might get there?" Or perhaps you are unsure about the direction for the company; then you might say, "I am not sure about our next steps as a company. I would like to share with you all where I am in my current thinking and would like to get your thoughts as we plan this together."

Remember, no one is expecting you to always have all the answers, but they are expecting you to be transparent, decisive, and inclusive. A leader who has these attributes at a minimum will have a higher likelihood of attracting and retaining great talent, which is what you will need to be a successful leader of your own company.

LEADING IN AN ESTABLISHED ORGANIZATION

Now that I have covered a few points that should be helpful if you are leading a company you've created, let's discuss how you choose a team if you're working within a corporate environment. If you are a rising leader within an organization, you will inherit a team and may be faced with making personnel changes to it. Most times, it is not wise to fire all the existing employees and start fresh with a new team. There are probably at least a few people on the existing team that know more about the organization and what needs to be done than you do. As a new leader, you must take inventory of your team members' portfolio of skills, assess their roles, and determine if they are great contributors or not. Then you have to compare those skills to your future strategies and plans for the organization.

It is also wise to assess the attitudes that prevail within your team. Who has a constructive, can-do, "willing to try all things new" attitude? And who has a "Dr. No, tried it before, stuck in their ways, here we go again" attitude? As you observe people who are unwilling to engage with your vision as a leader, you must act quickly to remove them from your team. As a new leader, your success will heavily depend on having a team that you can trust, that is constructive, and that wants to support your vision and strategy. In addition, you do not have to worry that if you have to make some organizational changes, it will be viewed as disruptive. It is generally expected that when a new leader arrives, there will be some organizational changes. Use the "air cover" of being new to make the changes you need for moving forward. If you wait too long, it could be more difficult to make changes or there could be repercussions for some of the decisions you make.

As a new leader within an organization, you will usually have the latitude to hire at least a couple of new people to assist you with the execution of your vision. If you are coming into an established organization as the new CEO or senior leader, it would not be unusual to bring over a few people from your old organization after a period of time. You want to be extremely thoughtful about your timing when bringing in people from your old organization because if people in the new organization feel threatened, they might be motivated to leave, and you could lose valuable intellectual and experiential DNA. If you have been asked to lead an area within your company that you have never led, you must quickly assess who on your inherited team knows the most about the department or organization, and you want to partner with that person right away to learn as much as you can in the shortest time. The easiest way to work with them is to admit what you don't know and your desire to invest in their success as they invest in yours. You must establish a mutual agreement that is transparent about your need to gain an understanding of the organization or department from them and their need for you to reward them or invest in their success going forward.

LEADERSHIP GEM:

When you are building your team, consider a potential employee's skills, aptitude, appetite to learn, pivot, and problem solve, and attitude. It is also important that you understand how they will fit in with the team and the company culture.

As you move to build your team, I want to caution you about one common pitfall. If you are now leading an area where you have very little previous exposure, beware of hiring someone just because they have more experience in a particular area than you have. You may have a tendency, as I did, to place a super premium on the person's skills and knowledge because you do not have that particular expertise, and you may not pay enough attention to the other needs you have around their work ethic, willingness to think creatively, or desire to leverage external relationships. I also did not properly value my own ability to learn quickly, my extensive network of internal and external relationships, and over twenty years of financial services experience. As a result of making this hire and not giving myself enough credit as an experienced leader, the results that the team produced were less than stellar and took almost eighteen months longer to produce.

MOTIVATION

As a leader, how do you motivate people? How do you keep people motivated? If you want to be an impactful leader, you must consider that it is your job to keep your team motivated to execute their roles. Many leaders assume that the money or the title will be enough to keep people motivated, but it is not enough, not in a labor market as tight as the one we are experiencing. Given the generational and demographic shift that is taking place in the world, the money or titles are not enough to keep great talent in your organization. Today's professionals want to be motivated and feel inspired when they go to work every day. As a leader now, you must embrace that it is part of YOUR duty to create that motivation.

In a very gross generalization, I believe that most people are motivated by three things: money, title/promotion, or the public "atta boy or atta girl." As a leader of an early-stage company, you want to try to figure out which one of these is the primary driver for the person you are hiring to be a part of your immediate team, because you must assess whether you or the organization has the capacity to deliver these things to keep your new senior talent motivated enough to stay with you, at least until they help you to reach key milestones. Remember, it's not just about what you have to offer today but what you can keep offering and delivering through these milestones of value creation for your company.

As a leader in an established organization, you must engage with your team quickly to understand what motivates them. There is, frankly, no substitute for taking the time to engage with people to understand what motivates them. Obviously, people do care about money, but it is not the only driver. I have found that while people do care about their compensation, they also value being formally and informally recognized for their work. They care about being included in key decisions, being asked for their opinion. Some professionals care about days off or flexibility in how and when they get their work done. You are going to be far more effective as a leader, gain the respect of your team, and retain your best people and attract new ones if you manage each key relationship by leveraging what motivates them most, beyond their primary monetary compensation.

One of the greatest leadership lessons I have learned is how much people value it when you invest in them, their career, and their success.

When you take the time as a leader to understand your team's development needs and design opportunities and projects that allow them to learn and develop expertise, they not only appreciate it, but it creates an undefined bond. It is very hard for someone to leave an organization when they feel that a leader in the organization is investing and has invested in their success. There are two things at play here. First, when you support someone, you create a sense of loyalty, a sense that they somehow owe you for what you have done for them. Second, they implicitly understand that if they stay, you are likely to keep investing in them. Taken together, these are two powerful motivations to stay with the organization. Last, don't underestimate the fact that people like to work with people they enjoy, feel admiration for, or just like being around. While we don't often talk about the "likability" factor in leadership, it is a powerful tool to motivate and retain great talent.

If you can help others understand what their career trajectory looks like in your organization, that is also a powerful tool for retaining your best talent. Here is where I see clear generational differences. Most Boomers and Xers did not get clear direction on the various twists and turns that were created in their career, and they learned how to be uncomfortable working in obscurity. I don't mean to imply that they functioned in total darkness, having no idea of their career trajectory. In most organizations, it was clear that a manager role was generally followed by a role as vice president, followed by a role as senior and executive vice president respectively. In an investment banking setting, the sequence was associate, vice president, executive director, and then managing director. What was not clear was which of the various roles and responsibilities you might have to shoulder within each of these levels. As I said earlier in the book, Millennials and Gen Zers highly value transparency. The more transparent you can be about your or the organization's intentions for their careers and the direction they will take, the more likely they are to be motivated to stay with you or your organization.

If you have invested in someone's career and you can articulate your continued intention to do so, chances are you will also have a reputation in the industry for being that kind of leader. Great candidates will be highly interested in working with and for you and, more important, in staying with you. As the old saying goes, people rarely leave organizations, they leave people, so you want to be known as that person who will invest in others!

CHAPTER 4

Embracing and Taking Risks

LEADERSHIP PEARL #4:
Fear has no place in your success equation.
Leaders take risks to grow.

STUDY THE CAREER journey of any successful leader, assess their failures and successes, and you will find they have one thing in common. Successful leaders are risk-takers. Whether it's exercising their voices to speak up in internal meetings about critical, strategic decisions, giving their clients difficult or unsolicited advice, investing in expensive technologies or processes, hiring senior people, or speaking up on behalf of others, strong leaders routinely take risks by stepping outside their comfort zones or making big bets on decisions that could be pivotal for their companies. These are the people who take on an international assignment, often leaving family, friends, and their internal career support behind. These are the people who take on turnaround assignments, start new divisions, close plants, and speak truth to power, even when leadership is not easy to approach.

In my book *Expect to Win*, I defined three types of risks: calculated, studied, and step-out-on-faith. To be a powerful and impactful leader, you must not only know how to identify these risks; you must also have a strategy for when to act on and how to use each one.

I have seen many smart, outstanding professionals with all the right skills and credentials fail to move to the next level of professional

65

achievement and leadership because they fear failing. Rather than take the necessary risks to move ahead, they merely accept where they are and rationalize that something or someone will come along and eliminate the risks associated with moving forward and clear the path for them to move ahead.

I once had a conversation with a newly minted CEO of a Fortune 500 company. He shared with me that even though he had been working for his entire thirty-year career to get to the top spot, he had so much reticence about taking on the role that he almost didn't accept it! When I asked what he could possibly have been worried about, his answer? "The risks of being a CEO."

He explained, "As the CEO, everything that I do is public. If I make a bad decision, the board knows it, the employees know it, my direct reports and people in the marketplace know it. For example, if the decision negatively impacts the stock price over a sustained period of time, it could not only cost me my job, but given the high-profile nature of the seat I'm in, it could finish me professionally. If you take a risk, Carla, maybe try a new opportunity and it doesn't work out, then you can move to another project, another department, or even another company. But as CEO, I don't have that luxury."

While much of his argument may have been true, he eventually moved past the reticence by reminding himself that he was a smart man with thirty years of experience. "I may not have seen every possible scenario that could occur at this company," he said, "but I have a track record of taking calculated risks. I have confidence in my ability to think and problem solve, and more important, as CEO, I have easy access to the best minds in this company and access to industry leaders whom I can consult for help. I have been in tough spots before and successfully managed my way. I have that survivor instinct, and if I have done it before, I will be able to do it again."

With a little analysis, he was able to embrace the risks associated with the top job and take on a terrific opportunity for himself and the company. He became one of the best CEOs in the company's almost century-old existence, making strategic decisions that were transformative for the organization and setting it up as a leader in its industry for another decade.

Just like that CEO, you must learn to review, accept, and trust your own data and track record. As a professional, you've already accomplished many firsts in your life. When in school, you completed a research paper and studied for and passed major exams for the first time. You spoke in front of a group of people for the first time. You started friendships and built relationships for the first time. You graduated from college, and perhaps graduate school or some other form of additional education. You landed your first job and subsequently took on your first set of assignments. You, too, have a track record of successful firsts. You have done many, many things for the first time and done them successfully. Why would you doubt that you could do it again?

Oh, and by the way, you have also done things that haven't worked out. If you are human, you have been disappointed. But the truth is, if you are reading this book, you have recovered and lived to talk about it! More important, you learned something from it, and that learning has impacted and positively informed every "try" since. Taking the risk, even when it doesn't work out the way you wanted, always brings you the gift of experience, and experience is extremely valuable to a professional in general, but in particular to a leader.

I speak at conferences and seminars around the world and enjoy chatting with audience members. I often meet people who want to move on to bigger and better roles. When I ask them why they don't just go for it, at first glance, they typically have very rational, articulate reasons for not moving ahead. However, once I start digging a little deeper into their well-presented arguments and offer a counterargument of my own to their rationale, one element more than any other is usually the reason for their reticence. No matter what their gender or whether they are senior or junior, at the bottom of all the reasons why they don't "go for it" is FEAR.

Fear is one of the biggest obstacles at the core of why people don't move ahead in their careers, and particularly for individual contributors who want to ascend to leadership positions.

LEADERSHIP GEM:

The way you get more comfortable with taking risks is to take risks.

THE FOUR FEARS

There are four categories of FEAR: Fear of Failure, Fear of What Others Will Say, Fear of Success, and Fear of Limited Chances.

1. Fear of Failure or Making a Mistake

The number one reason I hear people give for not taking risks is that they are deathly afraid of failure. I find this fear particularly peculiar. Everyone fails at some time at something. Whether it's a relationship gone bad, an interview for a job you didn't get, trying to ride a bike for the first time, answering a question in class, there's something you wanted in life that you didn't get. So what is the big deal about failing?

When I consider my own career, I've failed plenty. But every time I failed, I learned something, usually something valuable. Through failing, I have learned things about my craft of being an investment banker, I have learned about myself—how I react to pressure, what happens when I fail to properly prepare, how I should behave in a successful relationship—or I've learned how to do something new.

In fact, I've learned more from my failures than I have from my successes. I'd also say the same of my colleagues and other people I've seen take risks and fail. Many times, they ended up in bigger jobs, or were hailed for stepping out of the box and taking a chance on behalf of the company. Taking a risk and learning the lessons gleaned from it have far greater value than any *potential* failure.

People often view the stakes at risk as being too high. Most professionals believe, especially in the early stages of their careers, that failing on the job could cost them the job. But in my experience, it is not the instance of failing that hurts you but rather how you message it, how you own it, and, more important, how you move on from it.

One of the biggest mistakes I ever made happened shortly after I joined the equity capital markets team and started pricing deals on the syndicate desk. It took me two years after moving to the team to earn a spot on the syndicate desk, which prices every equity deal that a firm executes on behalf of clients.

One day, I was asked to price a deal for an industrial company. The day before, my colleague had successfully priced a deal using a naked short strategy. *Naked short* is a term used to describe the difference between the amount of stock an underwriter *buys* from a company when the company is issuing stock to raise capital and the amount the underwriter *sells* to investors. The amount the underwriter oversells is called a naked short.

To distribute shares to the investors the underwriter sold to, the underwriter must buy these additional shares in the open market. Underwriters use this strategy when they suspect that there will be more selling interest than buying interest in the stock after the deal is priced, therefore putting downward pressure on the stock price. When the underwriter buys the stock in the open market, thereby "covering" the naked short, it offers support to the stock price to either stay steady at the deal price or slightly above, unless the selling interest is markedly greater than the buying interest. This is typically a "tool" used to support a deal price so that it does not go below the price of the original transaction.

The truth is, I did not understand the concept of a naked short and I certainly did not understand the strategy of when to use one. But nevertheless, I decided, like my colleague, to use this strategy when I priced and distributed the deal I was working on.

The only time the syndicate deal captain should include a naked short is if the demand for the original deal is somewhat weak and the deal captain suspects there is likely to be substantial selling pressure from current stockholders in the market the next day. In other words, if on the day after pricing, there are more investors looking to sell the stock into the liquidity created by the new deal and there is not enough demand to buy the stock, then the price of the stock will go down. In fact, it is highly likely that it will go down below the price of the new deal. In general, that is the last thing you want to happen if you are the underwriter. It looks bad for the company, your client, and the unhappy new investors who bought and own the stock, for they now own stock that is worth less today than it was yesterday!

If, on the other hand, a deal is strong and there is much more demand for the stock than the underwriter is buying from the company, then there is no reason to put a naked short in place. The demand is a reasonably sure sign that there will be more interest in buying the stock than there is in selling the stock, and the price in the aftermarket is likely to rise.

When it was time to price and distribute my deal, I thought to myself, "Well, he went naked and everything went well with his deal, so I'll go naked, and my deal is sure to do well, too." At the time of pricing, my deal was way oversubscribed, which was a very good sign that there would be a lot of demand for the stock in the aftermarket. Further, it was not only likely that the deal price would be strong, but it was also likely that the stock price would even rise above the deal price. Investor demand would most likely drive up the stock price the next day. In addition, if the underwriter chooses to use a naked short, the underwriter can never step in front of investors to buy the stock. That meant if I were to use a naked short, I would have to wait until the investors bought the stock before I could buy the stock to cover the short, at which time the price might be much higher and would cost my firm a substantial amount of money to cover the short.

The next day, the stock opened, and the price shot straight up like a rocket! Unfortunately, I had a very hard time buying the stock to cover the naked short. The price kept moving upward. It was clear that I had made a huge mistake! I would even say that it could be classified as a debacle! On the first day of trading, one of the senior managing directors made a big deal about what a huge mistake I had made. He walked around, talking aloud to anyone on the trading floor who would listen about how it was going to cost the firm a lot of money, asking how could this happen? Blah, blah, blah.

Now, mind you, he never spoke to me directly. But everyone knew he was talking about ME! On the second day of trading, I still had not covered the short. And once again, he walked around the trading floor ranting and raving about how expensive my error would be for the desk, the department, and ultimately the firm. It was at this point that I started to think to myself, "This could be a career-limiting situation; I need to do or say something."

On the third day, he started his tirade again. But this time I approached him and said, "May I speak to you for a moment in the conference room?" We stepped inside and I closed the door behind us. "I wanted to speak to you because I have heard you talking to people about the huge mistake that I made in pricing a couple of days ago," I said. "I clearly did not understand what a naked short was, and I admit that it was a HUGE error on my part. However, I want to assure you that I now know what a naked short is. In fact, I know what a naked, half-clothed, fully clothed short is! I also want you to realize that when I make a mistake, it is the exception and not the rule. I am very certain that nothing like this will ever happen again. I also know that you have my best interest at heart, so we don't have to ever talk about this incident again, right?" and then I looked him in the eye and smiled. That was the last time I ever heard him mention it!

I learned a lot from this experience. First, I learned that if you don't know something, ask somebody. There is no shame in that. Yet we are often so afraid to admit what we don't know. This especially holds true for those in senior positions or roles. Remember, no one can know everything. Just because you need help with one or two things does not diminish your power, strength, or authority. In fact, you exhibit leadership and confidence when you have the courage to ask questions or ask for help.

Second, I learned that if you make a mistake, own it! Never let anyone else control the narrative about you. I should have been the one making a big deal about this mistake to my colleagues right there on that trading floor. By doing so, I would have diffused anyone else's power over my situation.

Third, I learned that when you see a bully, call him out. Let them know, "I see you." When you call a bully out, you take away their power.

It was a huge mistake, but I lived to fight another day. The mistake was not career limiting, but rather, it became a very useful skill in my tool chest. I went on to become one of the top members on the syndicate desk, with my clients and colleagues alike routinely praising my work. Trust me, I know it feels awful to make a mistake, but by owning it, you keep your power and control over what people say about it.

LEADERSHIP GEM:

When you let others use your mistakes against you or use them as a reason not to give you new assignments, roles, or promotions, you are giving away your power.

Everyone makes mistakes. You can use the mistakes you make as leverage in your next assignment, because you now have experience and knowledge that you did not have before, and you can use them when you come up against your next challenge to influence your next success.

It is the same pearl that applies if one of your endeavors does not pan out. YOU should own the outcome, be the first to articulate it along with an alternative solution if one applies. I applied this pearl in the third quarter of 2012. In 2008, I took the first intrepreneurial risk of my career. I left my senior role in capital markets, where I had been very successful for almost twenty years and was known as an impactful senior leader, to help the firm start and introduce an emerging manager fund to the marketplace.

The term *emerging manager* is most commonly used to describe asset management firms that were founded and run by fund managers who were women and/or of African American, Hispanic, or Asian descent who managed capital across all asset classes—equity and fixed income.

The emerging manager sector had long been plagued with the challenge of achieving size and scale because large asset allocators like public pension funds and large private endowments, such as universities or Taft-Hartley funds, were reluctant to allocate large amounts of capital to smaller managers. Many had a rule that they would not, as an investor, represent 20 percent or more of a manager's "assets under management" (AUM). I had the idea that if we could raise a fund that would allocate to and invest in these smaller managers, we could catalyze other investments in them. This could fundamentally change the way these managers were viewed and invested in by the asset allocator community.

While we made tremendous inroads into that community, had very constructive, transformative conversations with large pension and endowment funds, and connected with many, many emerging managers, we ultimately were not successful in raising the fund. Why?

First, because when I set out to develop the fund and its investment thesis in early September 2008, THE financial service crisis of the last fifty years began in the third week of September. Investors of every kind were focused on trying desperately to protect all their assets.

Second, serious conversations with potential investors didn't start until mid-2009, and the risk appetite of the institutional investor community had declined significantly, particularly for private equity structures like ours.

Third, I had no idea that if you are a team seeking to raise capital for the first time, having never invested together as a team, most investors are unwilling to allocate money because, as a group, you have no history of successful investing. Additionally, if you are bringing a concept to the market for the first time, it is very difficult to raise capital because no investor really wants to be the first one in on a brand-new strategy.

Fourth, we were introducing an investment product to the market in a structure that had never existed before. In essence, it was a "first-time fund with a first-time product," and very difficult for asset allocators to embrace. A first-time team with a first-time fund was destined to have a completion challenge and under ordinary circumstances would face hurricane-force winds of resistance, not to mention the winds associated with a financial services crisis. In addition, we faced changing legislation (the Volcker Rule, which applied to our fund, and our firm was completely overhauled) and an overallocation to private equity by large public and private pension funds, a scenario created by the market meltdown, making it highly unlikely they would make a new allocation to a private equity fund.

After almost two years of marketing the fund, I had to tell my boss there was no deal to be had in this market environment. I was fully satisfied that we had spoken to every reasonable investor that could potentially lead this investment and make the fund successful. I listed the reasons they were not willing to invest and recommended that we suspend our efforts. I offered my recommendation on how we could message it to those who had invested in the fund and to the broader marketplace, how we could preserve our options to come back into the market at a later time, and how we should proceed based on what we now knew about investor interest and preferred structure.

My boss was very appreciative of how I handled the situation and the recommendations I made, as were the limited partners who had agreed to invest. As a result, he remained a huge buyer of Carla Harris as a leader and was supportive as I embarked on my next role at the firm and, ultimately, of my ascension to a vice chair at the firm.

In addition, as evidence that the marketplace accepted our message about not completing the fund, one of the investors still believed in our investment thesis and proposed structure. The fund fit perfectly with their goals as a corporation. Despite the change in legislation and market sentiment, they requested we accept a portion of their original commitment to invest into a separately managed account using the same strategy. It was a huge win for the firm!

Looking back on this experience ten years later, I continue to believe this risk was important for me to take in my career. Even though we did not complete the fund, the benefits of taking the risk are evident and did not deplete my potential legacy in any way. In *Expect to Win*, I share the three questions that anyone, an early-stage professional or an established leader like me, should ask when considering taking a risk.

The first question: *Will the risk potentially give you skills and experiences that you would not get in your current seat if you stayed over the next twelve months?* At the time I made the decision, I thought the financial services crisis would endure for a couple of years and it would be unlikely that I would have new deals to work on, or at least deals that would have been markedly different from those I had done in the past. Given the negative impact the financial services crisis had on the overall market, very few deals were being executed at the time, so if I had stayed in my role in capital markets, I would not have had the opportunity to add anything to my intellectual or experiential tool chest.

Alternatively, in the first six months of working on the new fund, I learned a tremendous amount about the investment management world, including how and why asset allocators make the investment decisions that they do; the most important criteria they consider when choosing an investment manager; and the role of consultants in the assignment of investment managers, among other important lessons. I learned about a completely new and large vertical of financial services, one I had not been exposed to in what was then two and a half decades in the industry.

The second question: *Will the risk expose you to people, relationships, and networks that you would not get if you remained in your current seat for the next twelve months?* Even though I could not see how bad the financial services crisis would be, I knew at the time that I was making the decision that I would have to approach and build relationships with pension funds, endowments, and Taft-Hartley funds, classes of investors to which I had no previous exposure. No matter what might happen, getting exposure to new classes of investors would be a value add to my career as an investment banker. As I mentioned before, there were no deals being regularly executed in the market during the first couple of years, 2008 and 2009, of the financial services crisis. As a result, I would not have added any new C-suite client relationships to my network. However, in having those early exploratory conversations with asset allocators and even in formally marketing the fund, I built meaningful relationships with CIOs, state treasurers, city officials, corporate CFOs, and other leaders in the institutional investor community that I had previously never had exposure to. I was also able to introduce other leaders within the firm to some of these key decision makers, which resulted in ongoing engagement and business for the firm. In addition, after the capital markets recovered and investing in emerging managers increased, we were invited to compete for some of those emerging manager investment mandates, which led to increased assets under management in our alternative investments area.

The third question: *Will taking the risk create new branches on your personal "decision tree of opportunities" going forward? In other words, will you be able to pursue opportunities or do things that you would not be able to do if you stayed in your current seat for another twelve months?* If I had stayed in my capital markets seat for another twelve months, given no new deals, no new client relationships, no new deal structures introduced to the market, I would not have had access to any opportunities different from what I already had. As I moved into the investment management space, I not only learned about an entirely new vertical within financial services, I learned enough over the course of that experience to feel fairly confident that I could lead an investment management firm!

As I "raised my hand" to take on this exciting new opportunity, there was no question this was a significant risk for me and my legacy. My reputation as a very successful capital markets banker in mergers and acquisitions and capital markets was known inside and outside the firm. But if I had not taken the risk, allowing the fear of what could happen to my legacy as a successful investment banker/capital markets leader to take over, I would have missed the opportunity to acquire all the aforementioned knowledge, skills, and relationships that I could later use to further leverage my success at the firm. The key to preserving the legacy and leveraging the experience was in how I managed the experience, fully owning the good, the bad, and the ugly, and articulated the message when it was time to "call a thing a thing," when it was clear that we would not successfully complete the endeavor.

2. Fear of What Others Will Say—Legacy and Diversity

In order to lead effectively, you must free yourself from the fear of what others will say. In my conversations with leaders, particularly during the COVID-19 crisis and social unrest resulting from racial inequities in the United States, it is clear that many leaders know what actions they need to take to create more inclusive working environments. They know what they need to do to spur a greater level of innovation. But they are concerned about how internal or external stakeholders will respond and what they might say about their actions. This is particularly true with respect to actions related to diversity, equity, and inclusion, which was greatly emphasized in the aftermath of the murder of George Floyd in May 2020.

I have spoken to countless numbers of leaders of all ethnicities and genders. Interestingly, male leaders who are aware that their company cultures are suboptimal—that is, not inclusive and don't accommodate or encourage everyone to fully contribute—have been the most fearful of making changes. They are almost paralyzed by the fear of what others will say if they attempt to make the kind of changes necessary to yield lasting, sustainable results.

In a conversation with a white male CEO of a Fortune 200 company about how to communicate the imperative for diversity to the senior managers who reported to him, he asked me, "Carla, what do I do about the white male problem? If I tell staff about the kind of people changes that you are suggesting, I am going to hear from them. They will wonder, *What does this mean for me? What does this mean for my career?* How do I get people to get on board?"

I must admit that I was somewhat taken aback at the frankness of his question. It was clear to me that he wholeheartedly believed that if he could successfully implement cultural changes designed to create a more inclusive environment, his organization would be stronger for it. Still, his fear of not having the proper response had stopped him from moving forward with diversity, equity, and inclusion (DEI) for the four years he had been CEO.

Even he, like his senior leaders, was in effect hostage to the misperception that creating equity for all is a zero-sum game. He was unclear about how to create access and equity for one group without taking something away from another. That exact fear is what has created an obstacle to change in most organizations around the world. Personally, I believe he feared if he failed to have an answer to the question, he would lose his ability to get them on board with the corporation's DEI efforts as well as lose his standing with this powerful group.

LEADERSHIP GEM:

Inclusion is not about taking away from one group to give to another. Expanding the team to include people with diverse perspectives, backgrounds, ways of thinking, and problem-solving skills is the key to creativity and market-leading innovation. You cannot have sustainable innovation without successful inclusion.

"When you are asked, *What about me? Why should I embrace this?* or *How will these efforts benefit me or my team?*" I explained to the CEO, "Here is what you say . . . Let's call this person Fred. Fred, I understand that you don't see the benefit of our diversity and inclusion efforts, but I believe they will allow us to get greater overall contributions from all of our people. We must create an environment where our diverse colleagues feel that they have equal access to opportunities within the firm and that their voices and contributions are highly valued. When we establish our reputation as a diverse, equitable, and inclusive employer in the marketplace, that only improves our ability to attract other great talent from diverse backgrounds. As we know, studies show that diverse teams perform better, are more innovative, and have a greater impact on the bottom line. This will result in a higher return on the technological and operational investments we have made, produce greater revenue and profit, and result in higher retention among our organization's best people. Plus, it will produce greater value for our shareholders, and don't forget, we are both stockholders. Further, it will also mean better compensation for you and me.

"If I am right, Fred, the pie gets bigger for all of us. Here's what I am asking you to do. For the next two quarters, you don't have to participate in any of our efforts, but I'm asking you not to get in the way. I don't want to hear any negative talk or body language when the subject of DEI is raised, NOTHING. Right now, you have one-eighth of a twelve-inch pie. But if I am right, the pie will get bigger for all the reasons I mentioned, and then you will have one-eighth of a sixteen-inch pie. By definition, your one slice will be more valuable. If I am right and we start to see the kind of results I predict, then I will expect you to be all in and fully embrace, support, and promote our DEI efforts. If at that point, you still do not feel you can, then we must have a different conversation. Do we have a deal?"

"Carla, that is the best explanation I have heard to date," said the CEO. "I will deploy your 'pie' argument and let you know how it works out." A few months later, he called to report that Fred was fully on board and among the leaders who were promoting the CEO's vision for a more inclusive environment. My own "aha" moment from this experience was not only that this leader's fear was limiting his potential as a more powerful leader but that his lack of knowledge on HOW to execute was another obstacle to creating the change and unlocking the enormous potential in the organization.

I urge you as a leader to have the courage to leverage your relationships and ask for help on not just the "what," but the "how," particularly for topics like diversity and equity, which are often considered tough or sensitive. If you are a leader who has not had the lived experience that gives you insight into some of the more challenging DEI issues, then leverage the powerful experiences of those within your organization to better understand and develop a strategy to help your people navigate these sensitive waters. If this leader had not had the courage to ask a question that was clearly on his mind and was an obstacle to moving forward and making positive change for the company, he would not have progressed as a person or a leader.

If he had allowed himself to give in to the fear of what others would say, he would not have had the conversation with me and would have walked away without a possible solution for engaging his senior leadership team in his vision and for unlocking great potential in his organization.

Fearing what others will say is extremely tricky in today's environment. In the past, many companies felt strongly that speaking publicly about their views and challenges with respect to diversity, equity, and inclusion was not something they should do. Further, it was a common feeling that it was not appropriate for the company, its CEO, or other executives to take a position and talk publicly about important social issues. For example, in recent years in the United States we witnessed a rash of incidents of racial brutality against African Americans, Asian Americans, Jewish Americans, and other ethnicities; and several states have passed measures designed to make it harder for Americans, especially minority groups, the elderly, students, and people with disabilities, to vote, by changing voter ID laws, purging voter rolls, and more. In fact, many companies had policies in place forbidding executives as well as all employees from speaking out, feeling strongly that they should not publicize their support of these issues or of any organization committed to addressing them.

However, in 2020, we saw that change. Companies, and often their CEOs, started speaking out, sharing where they stood with respect to improving the state of racial affairs or other inequities in our society. What changed? Millennials and Gen Zers, who highly value transparency, have a strong appetite for voice . . . hearing a company or a leader SPEAK about issues that affected them as employees, as shareholders, and as community citizens. Suddenly, companies had to answer to these important stakeholders who demanded to know where companies and individual leaders stood on these issues. And the tool these groups most often deployed to make that demand known was social media. The demand for this corporate voice was so strong in

2020 that an organization's or leader's silence could be erroneously misconstrued and negatively impact their brand or market capitalization.

For the first time, we saw many leaders go public with their personal beliefs as well as on behalf of their organizations about where they stood on these issues. The year 2020 will mark the year when the fear of what others would say was outweighed by the fear of the potential ensuing ramifications of not speaking up about issues important to stakeholders. In the end, many organizations were rewarded with positive stock price reactions or greater philanthropic support for exercising their public voice on these issues. An important leadership pearl to embrace.

Voice is a powerful tool in driving change in an organization, especially cultural transformation, like developing a more diverse and inclusive environment. To be a powerful leader, you must be willing to embrace the risk of speaking up, especially internally to your employees and about issues you may not be comfortable with or have been exposed to.

LEADERSHIP GEM:

While it can be uncomfortable to exercise your voice around societal issues, like race, gender, and inequities, remember, there is no change without discomfort. Great leaders learn to get comfortable with being uncomfortable.

In 2020, as we moved from one terrible incident driven by racial inequities to another, I strongly encouraged C-suite leaders to embark on listening tours with their employees or to instigate what I called courageous conversations around topics including race, gender, and access to opportunities within organizations. There were many internal legal and HR leaders who were either against having these kinds of conversations or at the very least afraid to have them. But we had to acknowledge how the external environment and the world around us was clearly affecting the internal cultures of organizations across the United States. As disillusioned and disgruntled associates reported to their offices or teleworked using electronic platforms like Zoom and Microsoft Teams every day, many leaders took the risk and embarked upon a listening and learning journey. A year later, there is not one leader to whom I gave this advice who would not say that, while they still have a long way to go, their organization today is better because they started having the conversation.

Leaders feared having these courageous conversations not only because they worried about potential lawsuits or exposing the gaps in the company's HR policies and procedures, but also because they feared they might say the wrong thing, offend someone, or ask a "dumb" question. Leaders fear looking ignorant or inept. They fear misspeaking on these "sensitive" topics and having a mass revolt by one or more demographic groups. They fear their mistakes will be exposed on social media, cable news, or the front page of *The Wall Street Journal*. As a result of these fears, leaders who are otherwise very strong, decisive, and great at doing most things do not reach their full potential. They allow their fears to keep them from engaging in the kinds of conversations that would educate, inform, and inspire them to make the changes in their organizations. Changes that would result in more engaged, productive, and innovative cultures that would produce better results for customers and retain more people of color and women.

Again, I typically refrain from generalizing based on race. But, in my experience, while white leaders commonly fear what people will say, I have found that Black leaders have a different kind of fear under the same banner. Black leaders, including me, often fear what others will say if they simply express an opinion that is counter to the prevailing advice or opinion shared by most of their other colleagues or leadership. We tend to worry that others "might not like it" if we share our personal experience, or that of another person of color, that was unjust, unfair, or suggests an uneven playing field.

As we will discuss in chapter 6, one of the hallmarks of great leadership is exercising one's voice or, as I like to say, "calling a thing a thing." It is important that all leaders, but especially Black leaders, exercise their voice and speak up when they see or experience something they believe is wrong or inequitable. Failing to speak up and ask questions, not expressing that something matters to you, communicates to those around you that perhaps these things don't matter to you. If we, as Black leaders, are choosing to be in an environment, then it is important that we do our part to improve the environment by calling out those things that compromise any efforts that might create an inclusive environment. We should not be constrained by our forecast of others' reactions.

This is especially true when it comes to advancement in the workplace. I have learned the hard way, "If you don't ask, you don't get." As Black leaders, we must make sure to make clear our expectations about promotions, assignments, and opportunities. Far too many times, I have seen really great leaders of color across all industries, while waiting to move up the corporate ladder, tend to wait for someone to choose or promote them. And when things don't transpire as expected, they are disappointed, often disillusioned, and often leave the organization or settle for positions that do not allow them to put forth their best work. Instead, my advice, especially as a leader, is to ask the questions, "What happened?" "Why didn't I get that opportunity?" There is extraordinary impact when a leader asks the questions of the organization. It often exposes the inequities in the culture, which prohibit an organization from being as competitive as it could be in the marketplace.

Diversity, equity, and inclusion have historically been tough and uncomfortable topics for leaders, and the fear of addressing them and getting it wrong was previously greater than the perceived reward of doing so. On the one hand, I understand this perspective. Up until now, CEOs did not consider creating a more diverse and inclusive culture as something of paramount importance to their performance and legacy. In fact, most corporate boards previously treated the topic as a "nice to have" or the "moral thing to do" and did not hold CEOs accountable for meaningful cultural change as an evaluative parameter.

Most leaders approach the leadership seat with the objective of leaving the organization or company in a better position than they found it. When a CEO retires, they want to be able to point to the hallmarks of their legacy, achievements like a double or triple stock price increase, a successful merger, or double-digit revenue or profit growth. A college president wants to be able to point to record-breaking fundraising and new buildings as part of their legacy. A non-profit leader wants to point to a successful capital campaign, the increase in the number of employees in the organization, doubling the budget, or increasing the number of constituents served. Whether it is the board of directors who evaluate the CEO or the board of trustees who evaluate college presidents and philanthropic leaders, until recently, diversity, equity, and inclusion (DEI) were not among the top three evaluative parameters or contributors to a leader's legacy.

However, things have changed. In today's environment, a CEO's or any leader's legacy will be partly defined by how well they transformed and redefined the company's or organization's culture to one that is more inclusive and that embraces diversity. In the past, because DEI was not considered an important component of a CEO's legacy, one could argue that if the last three CEOs failed to make sweeping culture changes—like transforming the environment to be more inclusive—and the company survived, perhaps even thrived, then why should the current CEO endeavor to make these kinds of changes? Why take on the challenge with the risk of failure and impair one's personal legacy by focusing on these uncomfortable and sensitive topics?

Diversity and inclusion have previously been associated with fear. In the past, leaders convinced themselves that to do what was necessary for diverse and inclusive environments would require "massive change" that would be "difficult." After all, most people subscribe to the maxim that "change is hard," and before now, most corporate boards did not view creating an inclusive culture as a prerequisite for success or as a top strategic priority for the organization's future.

Now, however, we find ourselves in a very different environment. Inclusive corporate cultures have become table stakes for the new emerging majority in the workforce: Millennials. As we will discuss later in the book, this demographic demands three things from their workplaces at a minimum: transparency, inclusion, and feedback. When one or more of these requirements is not present, younger professionals won't likely join an organization. If they do join, they are not likely to stay once they figure out that the environment is not as they expected.

Therefore, leaders who fail to successfully bring their organizations through this transformational culture change and companies that do not have the agility to transform quickly to adjust to this new reality are going to find that they are no longer considered an employer of choice in their industries. Fear of what others will say or fear of impairing one's legacy is not a viable justification for this kind of failure.

Even leaders who feel comfortable navigating the path toward change and a more inclusive culture, and who can speak passionately about the topic of diversity and inclusion, compromise their effectiveness when they end well-written, inspiring speeches by saying, "It will take time. It's hard to do." When I hear this, I know that very little will actually get done toward making serious change while they are in the leadership seat. Because, in their eyes, it is too hard. They fear what others will say, and they believe there is too much at risk to their leadership legacy if they don't get it right.

In one-on-one meetings, when I have had the opportunity to ask leaders what they feel is the real impediment to change, they often have the same reply. "It is too hard. What will the board say about the changes if they don't work, if they cost us profits or revenues, or if I lose some great talent because of these changes?" During one of my conversations, the leader of a Fortune 250 company said, "We can't just snap our fingers and make everything equitable. These things take time. We can't just mandate that everyone behave in a certain way; you have to get people to buy in over time."

This leader did not buy into the strategic imperative of improving the culture, nor did he understand the connection between having a diverse group of leaders in the organization and the company's ability to compete in the marketplace. Needless to say, this organization has been moving at a glacial pace in driving changes and has lost a number of great women leaders and leaders of color. The company now has a reputation in the industry as not being a great place to work and has given up several points of market share to its closest competitor in the industry.

Leaders often feel horribly exposed as they navigate the journey of enhancing their cultures. They don't feel that there is the same type of "air cover" or support they would typically get as a leader trying to navigate a massive technological overhaul, expanding the footprint to a new country or geography, or even poaching a high-profile talent from a competitor. If they fail in any of these contexts, there is the air cover of the exogenous environment. For example, in competitive races for talent, everyone knows that one organization can outbid another and that they are not likely to just let their best talent walk out the door to go work for the competition. People acknowledge that technological transformations are fraught with risks, particularly people-related risks, such as having the *right* people to drive the transformation, or having people adopt the technology, etc.

Sure, if there were air cover for the risks associated with cultural change, leaders could potentially derive the courage to move forward, just as they do with technological changes. But with cultural transformations, since there is not a lot of evidence and data available that point to a model of success, leaders often feel that the risk of getting it wrong and the public exposure associated with this kind of change is just too large.

Now one of the advantages that we have from the environment in which we find ourselves, discovered from dealing with the COVID-19 pandemic and social unrest, is that it is exactly these types of environments that offer an enormous opportunity for change and support. One of my favorite sayings is "Chaos breeds opportunity." Given the chaos these two phenomena have created, an unprecedented opportunity has emerged for leaders to make the kinds of shifts they need to in their company cultures.

LEADERSHIP GEM:

Crisis and chaos often offer great opportunity to take substantial risks that result in meaningful change.

Both the pandemic and the social unrest have created air cover for leaders who want to transform or pivot their cultures without the typically associated risk of retribution. If a leader tries to make these kinds of cultural changes and they do not work, they can say, "COVID-19 created a unique environment that made execution difficult" or "the social unrest made it challenging to get widespread adoption." This chaos has created an environment where people are very willing to try new things, especially things that are marketed as productive, constructive, transformational, and advantageous.

3. Fear of Success

I clearly remember the first time I heard the phrase "fear of success." I wondered, "What is that? Why on earth would anyone ever FEAR success?" There I was at my alma mater, in Harvard Yard, listening to Dr. Matina Horner, then the president of Radcliffe College, as she gave a speech outlining some of the points from her recently published work about the fear of success. That was my introduction to the concept. I could not believe there was such a phenomenon—that someone could be so fearful of not being able to control an outcome or of facing negative reactions to success both personally and professionally that they would literally freeze and fail to move the project, idea, or process forward. It was strange for me to realize that what looked like procrastination might actually be terror.

I have had hundreds of conversations with professionals at various stages of their careers and met countless people who have had clear leadership abilities and aspirations to ascend in their organizations. But many of them have failed to do so because they feared that if they achieved success . . . well, then what? How would their coworkers, friends, and communities treat them? Would they be able to handle the requirements that the next level of their career would demand? What if people didn't embrace them in their new role? Some even failed to move forward because they were waiting for someone to give them permission or tell them that they could or should.

Derrick came from humble beginnings. Most of his family members and his neighborhood friends finished high school, but few pursued higher levels of education. Derek, however, earned his bachelor's degree from a prestigious four-year institution and landed a job earning a six-figure salary at a consumer packaged goods company. Derek received four promotions in his first five years at the company and was considered one of the organization's high-potential employees. He was clearly on the management track.

Derek was easily the most successful person in his family and among his friends. He wanted to make sure he didn't do anything that would take him off track in his career. One day, Derek's boss approached him about taking on a "stretch assignment." It would require Derek to learn new skills, gain exposure to senior management, and acquire new experiences. His boss made it clear that if Derek was successful in this assignment, he would be eligible for an early promotion to vice president, giving him increased management and profit and loss experience. Derek's boss also gave him the option of passing on the opportunity, continuing to do what he was doing. He was fairly certain that Derek would still be on track for a promotion "on time" in a couple of years.

While Derek was confident that he could execute the assignment, he was concerned that if he was promoted "early," he might not be ready for all the additional responsibilities and pressures that would accompany being a vice president. He didn't want anything to interfere with this current trajectory of success. Derek declined the opportunity and opted not to take the risk to accelerate his career. He chose to stay on his current track, where he thought, as his boss said, that he would be promoted in two more years. Because he did not know what to expect of an early promotion to vice president, he believed this was the better, safer option. Derek may in fact get his vice president title down the road, but what opportunities did he miss out on because he feared success? What could happen in two years, having nothing to do with Derek's performance, that could change the decision-making process? For example, what if there was a change in leadership or a change in the promotion process, such as different criteria?

4. Fear of Limited Chances

As an African American, throughout my life I've heard phrases such as "You have to be twice as good to get half as much" or "You only get one shot to make a mistake." In fact, most of the African American professionals I know, many who are members of the Baby Boom or Gen X generations, had these ideas drilled into their consciousness by well-meaning parents and mentors from the time they were children, and certainly throughout the early part of their professional careers.

After I joined the workforce, I also met women of color from other ethnicities who were indoctrinated with similar messages. When I reflect on my own personal history of risk-taking or lack thereof, I realize that my reticence or failure to take risks early in my career was rooted in the belief that I would not be given as many chances to make mistakes as my colleagues who did not look like me. It was my firm belief that I had to be very careful about what risks I chose to take.

There is no doubt, if someone believes that they will not be able to recover from a risk gone wrong or that any future opportunities to be successful will be thwarted, then no reasonable person would ever take a risk. The problem is, if you don't take risks, you won't LEARN how to take risks, and successful risk-taking is a learned behavior. Risk-taking is a muscle that you have to develop. If you don't learn how to take risks in the early stages of your career, then you won't develop a model for successful risk-taking, and it will impair your personal and career growth.

You won't develop a thought process or learn how to justify or refute risk-taking. You won't develop the confidence you need and sense of timing necessary to know when to take risks. More important, you won't learn how to recover from the inevitable mistakes that sometimes come with risk-taking.

And, as a result, you will spend an inordinate, exhausting amount of time trying to avoid making mistakes, which will impair your ability to create and innovate because you are focused on running out of what you believe are limited numbers of chances. As we discussed earlier in this chapter, this is particularly important because the ability to take risks is a key to being an impactful leader, especially today when innovation is a dominant competitive parameter across all industries.

Corporate cultures differ widely across industries, and some have more tolerance for mistakes than others. However, no matter what industry you work in, approaching your job or your career with a limited view of risk-taking because you fear making mistakes *is* a mistake. You must remember that making a mistake does not make you special. Mistakes happen to everyone. Everyone, at some point, no matter who they are, falls down. What makes you special is how and if you choose to get up! There is not one person who is currently sitting in the C-suite or any kind of leadership role who has not made a mistake, no matter what you perceive or even what they might say.

To be a successful leader, you should assume that you'll be allowed to make at least a few mistakes before there are likely any serious consequences. Approaching your role otherwise, playing it safe because you believe there are no opportunities to take risks, will fail to show your boss and the organization the full extent of your talent and will compromise your ability to succeed. Being preoccupied with limited chances won't offer you the opportunity to demonstrate your skills, abilities, and initiative. The reality is that you have more opportunity to take risks, fail, and recover than you think. The truth is, showing initiative is generally rewarded even if it turns out that it was not the right thing at the right time. Showing initiative doesn't typically limit one's career; it usually accelerates it.

FATIGUE

I don't often delineate my advice between women and men, because I believe the "pearls" are gender agnostic. However, there is one attribute that I believe plagues more professional women than men, and that's fatigue.

I have talked to scores of senior women across all industries who have arrived at that rung on the career ladder just below the pinnacle of success, only to watch them opt out of vigorously pursuing the very opportunity they've been working toward their entire careers! They simply sit back and let their dream job pass them by. They say out loud to their family, friends, mentors, and to themselves, "I am too tired."

Here is the reason why. Despite the fact that they have successfully managed their home life and selected the right team to drive success at work, the journey to the leadership seat has been arduous for many of these women. In many cases, it might have taken two or more years longer than some of their male colleagues to reach the same level. Or they may have had to make more sacrifices than their male peers in trying to build their careers while maintaining their personal lives.

As a result, rather than taking their well-earned run at the position they've wanted for so long, they run away from the opportunity because they perceive or believe that the same extraordinary effort that was required to get them where they are now will be necessary to get them to the next level. They are simply tired of the fight and don't believe they have the energy to pursue the top job because it has already taken such an extraordinary effort to get where they are.

The irony is, once you make it to the rung just below the top job, it takes just a fraction of the effort to push through to the next opportunity. When you get that far, you have already done all the heavy lifting. Getting to the next level requires just a slight push. All that it requires of you now is to leverage the relationships you have built and exercise your power and voice to ask for the opportunity.

My advice to professionals who find themselves saying, "I am too tired. I don't have the energy," is to get some rest!!! I don't say this sarcastically or in jest. If you find yourself feeling this way, fatigue is coloring your perspective. You will be amazed at how your perception, your will, and your appetite for success will strengthen after just a few days away from work and a few nights of some good sleep. Before you walk away from the opportunity you have worked all of your life for, talk to your mentor or sponsor and hear from an objective voice about the new opportunity and your ability to pursue it.

LEADERSHIP GEM:

Self-care is critical for maintaining the physical and mental health required to be a great leader.

What do you have to lose by going for it? If you fail, you are generally no worse off than if you had not tried. What have you been working so hard for, enduring all that you have endured? You have earned the right to ask for what you want and to exert just a little push to get it. If you push through, you will complete the journey going from FEAR to FATIGUE to FEARLESSNESS!

RESILIENCE—BOUNCING BACK FROM FAILURE

A common trait I have noted among great leaders is their resilience. They do not allow a mistake or even a failure to stop them from continuing to move forward. When you experience a failure (and everyone does), I like to say every experience gives you one of two things: a blessing or a lesson, and both are valuable; take them, and then move on.

Either you will accomplish that which you were trying to achieve, a blessing, or you don't and fail, but you still gain valuable experience that teaches you a lesson, something that you didn't know before and that informs what you do on the next try. If you aspire to be a powerful leader, the absolute worst thing you or anyone can do is to continue to dwell on a failure. Doing so for too long transforms the mistake from an experience into an obstacle. Once that happens, by definition, it keeps you from constructively reflecting on and learning from the experience. In fact, it will dampen your enthusiasm and potentially even stop you from ever getting up the courage to try again. People who are not quite ready to be a leader will often become so consumed by a failure that they overexplain what transpired or, worse, shrink away from their work environment, becoming extremely reticent to ever try the experience again.

Chad was given a very important, high-profile role on a new product team. If the product was developed on time, on budget, and successfully introduced to the marketplace, he was certain he would solidify his promotion to executive vice president. But due to a series of unforeseen circumstances (i.e., the chief engineer left the organization, a key material input was delayed by five weeks due to an order and delivery snafu, etc.), there were changes in variables that Chad did not foresee. The product introduction was delayed by almost three months and was largely considered a failure within the organization as the competition introduced a similar new product that was very well received by the market.

Chad was devastated. This was the first significant failure of his career. His entire demeanor changed. Once gregarious, he became withdrawn and quiet, rarely speaking up or contributing in meetings. He no longer assertively asked for new projects. He even walked with his head hung down, avoiding eye contact with his colleagues. As time went on, people stopped asking for his voice and input. Chad fell behind in his career relative to his peers who joined the organization around the same time he had, and he was overlooked for assignments and subsequent promotions.

LEADERSHIP GEM:

*The question is not **if** you will make a mistake, it is **when**. Mistakes will happen. Great leaders learn from them and apply what they've learned going forward.*

Chad could have taken another approach. When a mistake happens, leaders who take the time to stop and study what went wrong and consider what they could have done differently, and strategize how they can do better going forward, fare so much better. It has been said that one of the reasons Tiger Woods is such a great golfer and a leader in the world of golf is because he has "the ability to leave a hole behind." Meaning, when he does not dwell on a particular hole on the course, he does not take the experience of that hole into the next one. Tiger starts the next hole fresh, executing the very best he can instead of thinking about the mistakes he made on the last hole. There are many historical examples of leaders who enjoyed immense popularity and power, only to have a great fall and later emerge even more powerful than before.

A common thread among all leaders who have demonstrated amazing resilience, from sports figures to politicians to corporate CEOs—think Steve Jobs, Martha Stewart, or Lee Iacocca—is that when they experienced a failure, they took the time to consider what went wrong. They dispassionately assessed the situation and then, most importantly, got back in the game and tried again! They did not view their failures as the end of their careers or as something from which they could not rebound.

There are very few things in life that are irreparable. One of the mistakes that most of us make as emerging leaders is that we overthink situations, especially if we've made a mistake. Strong leaders spend less time beating themselves up for what went wrong and more time strategizing on how to be successful in the future.

CHAPTER 5

Leveraging the Power of Collaboration and Partnerships

IN THE 1980s and 1990s, one of the hallmarks of leadership for companies in almost any industry was to have a proprietary process or product. Companies would consistently strive to be the first to market with something created exclusively in-house, without any partnerships, and that was trademarked or included some kind of exclusive execution step, or "secret sauce."

In fact, offering something exclusive to the market enabled companies not only to gain outsize market share but also to charge premium prices, enhancing their profitability. For example, pharmaceutical companies would spend billions of dollars per year on research and development. They would win a patent and be the first to market with a drug, owning exclusive rights to produce the brand for forty years before any generic version could be manufactured as competition.

In the last twenty years, as disruption and innovation have become the dominant competitive parameters in the market, companies have started to take a different approach. Today, collaborating and partnering can get products and services to market even faster. By coming together and sharing ideas and resources, organizations are making it easier to lead the market by creating competitive protection. Most companies cannot afford to spend five to ten years creating a product or process to introduce to the market. Technological developments, market fragmentation, and the start-up economy have decreased the rate of innovation from ten years to five years down to barely twenty-four months today.

Think about your cell phone. You used to be able to own the latest version for five years. Now a new one is introduced every twelve to eighteen months. Consider the evolution of music products over the last forty years. We've gone from LPs (albums) and 45-speed records to eight-track tapes, to cassette tapes, to compact discs, to MP3s, to downloads, to streaming! You'd be hard-pressed to find a brick-and-mortar music store today. Coconuts, Sam Goody, Virgin Records, and Tower Records are now largely a thing of the past.

As we've seen tremendous change in the marketplace over the last two years, we've seen a change in leadership, too. The "build versus buy" decision for most companies has yielded to the "collaborate and partner" strategy. Today's great leaders are intentionally positioning their companies and themselves to form partnerships, collaborating with other leaders and boards of directors, because they recognize that they may not have all the talent they need in-house to maintain their lead market position or they may not have the capital resources to build themselves. This is particularly true as tough market environments deplete companies' financial, technological, and human capital resources. Yet companies are still expected to innovate and expand on their product offerings and customer penetration as well as deliver new products and services.

The financial services crisis, the COVID-19 global pandemic, and the racial inequities and social unrest in the United States and around the world have made collaboration and partnership a necessity for ongoing success. It's nearly impossible today for companies to go it completely alone. No one company today can move as quickly on its own as today's innovation demands.

Pottery Barn and Sherwin-Williams have collaborated to introduce their products to new consumers. Betty Crocker and Hershey have partnered as a way of leveraging each other's brand strength. Red Bull and GoPro have partnered to leverage each other's core competencies. For these partnerships to be mutually beneficial, company leaders not only have to like each other and work well together, but they must also trust each other so each can leverage the others' intellect and experience, and be open and committed to providing their own diligence and energy. Today's leaders must understand what it takes to motivate people internally and externally, they must have extraordinary communication and selling skills, and they must be willing to invest on behalf of the other companies to ensure their mutual success.

Part of what any board of directors considers as they are choosing a new CEO, or opining on other key leadership positions within a company, is the reputation a prospective leader has in the marketplace. If you as a leader are under consideration for one of the top jobs, the board will consider what kinds of relationships you have with key leaders at other companies. They will ask what the likelihood is that you will be able to bring those relationships to bear on the company's future success. The board will also want to understand whether you will be able to attract other key talent and leaders to the organization. If you are known as a great executor or idea generator but do not have a reputation for successfully building organizations and attracting and retaining great people, in this environment, you are less likely to get the affirmative nod than someone who is known for having these skills, all else being equal.

For many companies, the key pathway to growth is to buy smaller emerging companies, ones that are disrupting the industry and within a few market cycles have the potential to disintermediate larger, better-capitalized competitors. Since these smaller companies generally have products, processes, and technologies that are attractive to many large incumbents, there is often a competition among would-be acquirers. As a leader in this type of market environment, you want to be known as an acquirer of choice.

Being an acquirer of choice is not just about being the company that can pay the highest price but also being the company that is likely to add the most value to the organization and to the target management team post-transaction. It is important that, as the leader, you have a reputation of being fair, strategic, and focused on building value for shareholders, and that you are deferential to the target management team. In general, you want the marketplace to see you as a leader that is methodical about making sure the management team is not only well compensated, but that you value what they bring in the transition of the sale.

If your acquisition style is to bring management into the organization, you want others to know that you are someone who will give a representative of the new management team a seat at the decision-making table. You'll want to quickly integrate them into the acquiring management team. If you are acquiring a brand that you want to continue operating as it did before the acquisition, make sure you have a plan to allocate the resources they might need, and construct a strategy to accelerate the company's scale. Your primary objective is to ensure the acquired management team, the shareholders, and the marketplace feel that this new asset is in the best possible hands and that your company is the right acquirer. This will advance your reputation as the acquirer of choice, which will be critical to your growth strategy via acquisitions.

One of the things you should be aware of as a leader in an organization that is an avid acquirer is the fact that the early-stage company ecosystem, while large, is a small community. Many early-stage CEOs have been in business accelerators together. Many are in the same venture capital portfolios. Many even went to undergraduate or graduate school together. As a result, they routinely share information with each other, even about the conversations they've had with other CEOs.

As you move through your career, your reputation as a leader will grow and be known far beyond what you know or are even aware of. As such, it is important that you are intentional about how you show up, how you interact with others, and how you are viewed as an acquirer. Do you have a reputation for being thoughtful and paying full price? Or are you known for trying to lowball the companies you wish to acquire, or for using tools like earnouts as part of your transaction price, where you buy the company for a specified amount but hold a portion in reserve until the company meets certain milestones over a two- to four-year period of time? Or are you aggressive on non-economic terms, like the conditions for closing the transaction or the number of years management has to stay with the combined entity? How long do acquired teams stay with your company post-transaction? Do you give them some stability and earnestly try to incorporate them into your organization? Or do you use them for the transition and then cut them loose?

Chris was on the executive team of a major corporation, Company A. He had been with the company for fifteen years and was known in the industry as an amazing scientist. He was the author of several patents and had created a software program that had quickly become an industry standard. He also had a reputation in the industry as being difficult to work with, often openly challenging and berating his team members and regularly taking credit for others' ideas. Without warning, Company A's CEO abruptly left. The board had to choose another CEO quickly.

Sheila was the COO of Company A. While she was not a scientist, like Chris, she also had been with the company for fifteen years. She had risen through the ranks and had a reputation of being a great team leader. During her stint in HR, she was responsible for sourcing more than a dozen senior leaders in various areas of the company and had a strong reputation as well as a strong following within the organization.

Sheila was very active in the start-up community, volunteering with several accelerators as an officer on loan and working with companies to help them position their brands in the market and to grow their brand's value. In fact, Company A's latest acquisition was the result of Sheila's interaction with one of the well-known accelerators in the community. Sheila leveraged her relationship with the early-stage company CEO, introducing her to Company A's CEO. Sheila had a long conversation with Company X's CEO about how it could accelerate its value by connecting with Sheila's company and leveraging its ability to penetrate new customer segments.

Every major competitor in the industry wanted to buy Company X. The venture capitalists invested in Company X were very interested in getting liquidity and selling their entire interest at the highest possible price. However, Company X's management team was focused on continuing to build the company and had plans for several evolutions of its technology product. Each of the would-be acquirers could bring value to the company, but they had differing views about whether or how to integrate and leverage the existing management team.

Company X would markedly accelerate Company A's leadership in the industry. It was widely known that Company A was going through a leadership change. Company X was very clear that it did not want to be acquired by Company A if Chris was going to be the new leader. Once the board of Company A learned that Chris as CEO might be a negative factor in the negotiations to buy Company X, it tipped the decision in Sheila's favor, making her the new CEO. Sheila was able to help the boards of the two companies A and X construct an acquisition agreement that was of value to both parties in both price and the plan for integrating the new management team.

A colleague of mine serves as president of a large subsidiary within a Fortune 100 company. She is known internationally, specifically for her ability to listen and for her interest in learning from any- and everyone. In five years, this leader has successfully sourced and engineered over twenty acquisitions, adding over $20 billion of value to her company. Whenever the company acquires a new company, the management team has opted to stay with the larger entity for longer than originally agreed upon in the acquisition deal. Why? Because they wanted to be a part of her team. Her leadership style inspired them to want to do whatever they could to contribute to her success with acquiring their company! They also benefited intellectually, experientially, and financially from being a part of the entity she was building inside the large company.

This is precisely the type of leadership profile and reputation that you want to have in the market and in the current environment. Most large organizations will find that they *have to* partner, collaborate, and/or acquire other organizations as a part of their company's future growth strategy. It is very difficult for large organizations in isolation to have meaningful growth that the market will reward. The market will value your company if it demonstrates innovation. The market will reward you if you are engaging with your customers and have a unique value proposition among your competitors. Consequently, acquisitions have become an essential part of any successful company's growth strategy, especially large companies. If your company achieves a certain size and is no longer experiencing double-digit growth, then shareholders will expect you to incorporate partnering or acquisitions as part of your growth strategy.

If you are not perceived as a preferred acquirer, it will handicap your growth strategy.

If you are the leader of an emerging company, it will not be easy to acquire the capital or the people that you need to quickly scale. In many industries, the fastest way to accelerate your growth as a small, disruptive company is to partner with or be acquired by a larger organization that can increase the rate of scaling in your company, introducing you to new customer segments or providing you with the distribution that you need to accelerate your growth.

If you have a reputation in the marketplace as a leader who is difficult to deal with, does not integrate well with others, or is disruptive to people and networks, then you will not be attractive to some of the larger potential partners, which could compromise your efforts to grow your segment or company or to realize the value you have built. If the product or services that your company offers are so outstanding, then they might want the company, its assets, or intellectual property, but not want you!

No matter how you cut it, your reputation as a leader can make or break you in countless ways. Partnerships and collaborations are here to stay. If you are going to lead in an impactful way, you must build your leadership networks with competitors and new market entrants and establish and enhance your reputation as a partner.

CHAPTER 6

Being an Intentional Leader

LEADERSHIP PEARL #6
*You are not a leader because you have the title;
you must be intentional.*

I HAVE SPENT my career in finance in what is known as a "producer culture." In a producer culture, people are not awarded leadership positions because they are great managers or inspirational leaders but, rather, because they "put points on the board." Meaning, they drive revenue or profitability, or execute a big initiative. It is as if, because you have arrived at a point in your career where you show outstanding aptitude in your area of expertise, such as trading, sales, or investment banking, or you land a big client and make a lot of money for the firm, then it is assumed you are ready to and are therefore rewarded with the opportunity to manage and lead others.

We know that generating a lot of money for your company or consistently landing big customers takes a certain skill set. However, it is not the same skill set required to effectively manage and inspire people to be the best they can be. The reality is, in most industries, people are never trained to lead or manage people in a motivational or inspirational way. I would argue that in producer cultures like investment banking, or financial services in general, one's *experience* as a trader or banker does in fact *not* qualify them to manage and lead others.

Awarding people manager roles based on their producer-related expertise may have worked for the 1980s, 1990s, and even at the beginning of the millennium, but it does not work today. Millennials and Gen Zers now make up the majority of the workforce, and they demand leadership from the people they report to. They are not looking for just a manager. They ask for instructive and constructive leaders who embrace transparency, inclusivity, collaboration, and feedback as table stakes in the culture.

Just because someone is a great producer does not mean they will be a great leader. The same is true of extensive experience; having it does not mean you will be a good manager. I believe that some people are natural leaders. However, I also believe that anyone can learn to become a good leader or an exceptional manager. Further, you can lead from any seat. Leadership is not a title and your seniority does NOT determine your ability to lead.

In fact, no matter what you do for a living, you have to be intentional about showing up as a leader EVERY DAY. Leadership is an active state of being. Leaders motivate the best talent to stay and grow. They define, drive, and carry a culture and are the people whom others want to work for, be taught by, emulate, and ultimately become.

To be that kind of leader, there are eight things you must be intentional about every day. You must:

1. Be authentic
2. Build trust
3. Have clarity
4. Create other leaders
5. Focus on diversity
6. Be innovative
7. Create inclusion
8. Use your voice

BEING AUTHENTIC

In my book *Expect to Win,* I wrote that authenticity is your distinct competitive advantage. It is at the heart of your personal power and one of the key elements of impactful and influential leadership. As a leader, when you bring your authentic self to every situation or environment, you motivate and inspire others to do the same. When people feel empowered to be who they really are, they will always outperform. And when the people on your team outperform, that performance accrues to your status in the leadership seat. In other words, when the people on your team look good, you look good.

Authenticity becomes especially important, and is key to effective leadership, during times of crisis. The entire world sheltered in place during the COVID-19 crisis, and my phone began ringing off the hook. C-suite and other leaders were asking, *How do I lead at a time like this? How do I motivate and inspire my people when we're working remotely and not all in the same place? How do I speak to my people when there is so much uncertainty coming from both within and outside our company?*

As I said to them and continue to say now, in times of crisis, especially in environments characterized by gross uncertainty, loss, and tragedy, you as a leader must be visible, transparent, and empathetic. Your authenticity is key to your ability to successfully deliver each of these to your people. During these conversations, I wondered why so many of these leaders, who are generally great decision makers, were having such a hard time in this period. I realized that many have *never* been their authentic selves in their careers and certainly not as leaders.

Since early in their careers, they figured out what they needed to do, how they needed to speak and act, and for many years had followed a playbook before being elevated to a leadership position, without ever having stopped to define who they really were. There was a strategy and a formula, and they followed the prescription to get to the top. Now, however, we find ourselves in an environment where being who you really are is required to connect and lead people through uncertainty. There is no playbook for leading through a pandemic or extensive social unrest. During this time when authenticity was a more critical component of leadership than perhaps ever before, they genuinely did not know how to be authentic.

I'm often asked, "How do I bring all of myself to work with me?" In short, it begins with knowing who you really are. While this might sound trite and like a bunch of self-help jargon, it's surprising how many people have no clue who they are! Many people spend their lives "checking the box" related to what they are doing and rarely stop to ask themselves questions like *Why am I doing this job? Is this a career I really want to continue pursuing or am I doing this because my parents, mentors, friends, or society tell me I should?*

Being your true self, knowing who you are and what you want, includes understanding your strengths and weaknesses. Start by describing yourself in three words. Keep in mind, there is not just one you. We are all multifaceted. There is a pensive you, there is a funny you, there is a lighthearted you, there is an intellectual, argumentative, and collaborative you, too. If you find this exercise difficult or uncomfortable, I would highly recommend asking for help. You might approach a really good friend, preferably someone who knows you well, and ask them to describe you in three words. If you feel uncomfortable having this conversation with a close friend, there are personal courses, coaches, and even therapists who can help get you started toward getting a better picture of who you are. That self-awareness is key to being a great, authentic leader.

Once you get clear on all the facets that make up who you are, embrace them. That is how you show up as the authentic you wherever you go. When you are comfortable with yourself as a person and carry that authenticity with you, it makes it easier to relax and meet people as who they are, too. When you are preoccupied with who you *think* you need to be, what you *think* you need to say, or how you *think* you need to act, you can't be authentic. Being who you are frees up conscious capacity to focus on others. When you are authentic, you can't wait to see who you'll meet, what energy they bring to the situation, and then decide what facet of your authentic self you want to put front and center to make a connection.

Keep in mind, none of us is the same person today that we were yesterday; we change over time. I have a practice that I highly recommend trying at least once a year. Find a quiet place where you won't be disturbed and take a few hours to consider who you are. Ask yourself questions like *How am I different than I was a year ago? What has happened in the last year that has changed my views on certain subjects? What am I more tolerant of? What am I more conservative about? What new things did I learn about myself? What has surprised me about myself, my reactions, or my interactions?* Each year, I discover something new about myself, and as I evolve as a person, I evolve as a leader, and so will you.

Authentic leaders continually work to know and understand themselves, and as a result, they know how to show genuine interest in others, including their team's success as well as that of every individual member of the team. They embrace all of who they are, including their own strengths and weaknesses, and therefore can do the same for others, genuinely giving credit where credit is due and demonstrating empathy rather than retribution when the inevitable mistakes are made. Being an authentic leader will attract authentic people to your team. They will genuinely want to invest not only in your team's success but also in yours as a leader. Bringing your authentic self to the table builds trust, which is at the heart of any successful relationship. To be an authentic leader, you must be intentional about building trust.

BUILDING TRUST

No matter what the industry, today's winners and losers are defined by innovation. Whether it's retail, financial services, transportation and logistics, healthcare, you name it, the fate of every organization depends on if and how fast it innovates, implements, and executes. In this environment, as a leader, you will find yourself trying to accomplish things that have never been done before and leading teams of people when the way forward is not clear. While you may have a plan, you are navigating in uncharted waters and have no idea how things will transpire. To get your team fully on board and willing to follow you and execute in the unknown, they have to trust you. If your team trusts you, they will follow you no matter what, even though they do not have a model of what the outcome should look like or how, or if, they will be rewarded or promoted.

As a leader, how do you create an environment where your team, or anyone you work with, trusts you?

The answer is simple . . . you deliver, over and over again. You do exactly what you say you are going to do. Think about your life and the people you trust. Perhaps it is your barber, your deliveryman, the dry cleaner, your babysitter or nanny, the hostess at your favorite restaurant, or even your boss. If you trust them, it is because they have consistently delivered on the implicit or explicit contract that you have with them.

Your dry cleaner consistently does a great job pressing and cleaning your suits, most delicate evening gown, or tuxedo. The restaurant you frequent always delivers fresh, hot, and tasty food that is prepared just the way you like it, and with impeccable service. Your babysitter is always on time, shows up consistently, and is flexible to stay late when necessary. These people have all developed a track record of offering either exactly or more than what you expect, and therefore you trust that they will always do so.

Just as each of these relationships has earned your trust is exactly how you must intentionally build trust with your team. Again, you have to deliver consistently, over and over. For example, if you want your team to trust you as someone who can receive bad news and productively act on it, then whenever there is disappointing news for the team or something does not work out as the team expected, you have to demonstrate empathy and understanding each time. Even though they, and you, too, may be disappointed, you focus on the important lessons learned as well as how that learning can be applied to another try or to a different success in the future.

Another way to establish trust is to explicitly define what your team can expect from you and what you will deliver to or for them, and then consistently deliver on what you promised. For example, Riley, a colleague of mine, has a reputation as a great leader. When she formed her new team, she told them, "You can expect four things from me as your boss. First, I will always have your back. If something goes wrong, I am the person who will defend you until the facts are known. If it turns out that you were wrong, I am going to be the first to share that with you in a constructive way. Second, I will never shoot the messenger. I prefer to hear all news, good and bad. And if you share bad news, I am never going to 'shoot you' for bringing it to me; I prefer to hear it from one of my own. Third, I will always look out for your development. My job is to make sure that you learn something when you are working with me and that each year you become better. Or, if you leave, you leave ready to tackle new things in your next assignment. Finally, I believe in giving people ongoing feedback. You will never have to wonder where you stand with me. You will know if you are doing a great job or if I think that you need to step things up a bit. You will never get any surprises from me during your year-end performance review."

As she began working with the team, Riley did exactly what she said she would do. Her team member Jennifer reported to her that one of her investment proposals was declined by the capital committee. Since Jennifer had ultimate responsibility to see the deal through the committee process, it was essentially her fault. But Riley did not respond negatively. Rather, she sat down with Jennifer to calmly review what she thought went wrong. She also gave her the benefit of sharing the feedback she had received from one of the committee members.

Together, they developed a plan to revisit the committee in three months with a strategy to get the deal accepted. While it took two more attempts, Riley worked with Jennifer to get the investment proposal accepted.

In another instance, team member Todd, a young vice president, was accused by another department of not following through on a client request. The client was very angry with the firm and took their business to another bank. It was a VERY BIG deal and a serious mistake. Instead of joining the chorus of people who were blaming Todd for the loss, Riley called a meeting with both teams and pointed out all the ways the two groups could have better handled the client, including getting more senior people involved. Todd used the mistake as a learning opportunity and was more proactive going forward, eventually becoming one of the organization's leading client relationship managers.

CREATING CLARITY

In this era of innovation, it is your job as the leader to clearly define for the team where you are headed even though, as we've established, the way ahead for you and your team may not be clear. You cannot allow your team to work in obscurity, because they will not get very far. In fact, their humanness will make them fight against it. As humans, we tend not to want to go toward places that do not resemble where we have been before.

Sure, you may be fine traveling to a city or country where you have never visited before because you have done so countless times and survived. You *expect* that the new place will be like other cities or countries that you have visited. However, if you have no idea what the experience will be like, you don't know anyone who has ever made the trip before, and you don't have the benefit of anyone's counsel or perspective, would you really make the trip? While some people might venture forth, most would not.

The same is true of teams. Most people, when they don't know where they are headed, will simply just refuse to move forward, and for a team, that can be very detrimental. In order for your team to advance, even in the face of uncertainty and obscurity, you as the leader must provide clarity. You are the person who must determine and share *what* the mission is and *where* you would like to go to achieve it. If you can't provide clarity for the year, then you have to provide it for the quarter, the month, the week, or even the day!

When I created the Multicultural Innovation Lab for Morgan Stanley, an in-house accelerator that provides capital, content, and connections for multicultural and women entrepreneurs, it was the first of its kind. No other investment bank had ever built such a lab in-house. I had no playbook of how to do it. No other department within Morgan Stanley had ever built such a lab either. So I couldn't get direction or solicit advice from other colleagues. I not only had to recruit a team of people to help me, but I also had to give them a vision and a "strawman" of execution steps, a starting place for our plan of execution. Rather than present a full plan, I left room for my team members to add their suggestions and thoughts and to put their imprimatur on the plan as we moved forward. Frankly, there were many days when I had no clue of where we should go for the next month or even the next few weeks. But in those cases, I would focus on defining what we needed to do for the week ahead of us, and then everyone would go off and dive into their roles, contributing to the team's forward progress.

When you, as the leader, provide clarity, you offer your team

members a target to aim for. When people know what they are supposed to be doing, what they are "playing for," their individual competitive spirits will motivate them to outperform and exceed that
which is defined, and that outperformance will accrue to your status in
the leadership seat.

CREATING LEADERS

When you get to the leadership seat, you should be disproportionately
focused on creating other leaders. That is how you will amplify your
impact in the organization. If all roads lead back to you as THE rain-
maker, the only one who can do the job, then the organization's success
and yours will eventually be capped because you are just one person.

LEADERSHIP GEM:

As a leader, one of your most important jobs is to create other leaders.

The key to expanding your firm's market share or footprint, to
further penetrating your existing customer relationships, is to create
other leaders. You must intentionally invest your experiential and intellectual DNA in others, while also leaving room for them to innovate
and evolve the organization's existing platform. Those experiences and
assignments that allowed you to "cut your leadership teeth," or gain
experience as a leader, must be passed along to other potential leaders,
allowing them to do the same.

Releasing ownership of the tasks I felt I was very good at was
tough for me. I have been blessed with a great capacity to efficiently
multitask and still deliver at the highest level. When people gave me
new assignments, I would easily just add them to an already full plate,
simply because I could. I never had to give up any tasks to take on
more. But what I also never had was the white space to evolve into a

better leader. I was so focused on the tasks on my very full to-do list that I never had the opportunity to do any inventive, creative problem-solving, or to spend time thinking about what being a powerful, respected leader really looked like.

Then, one day, I heard the chair and CEO of my company say, "I focus on those things that only the CEO can do. If there is anything on my list that someone else could do, then it should not be on my list." I thought he was an effective leader, so his comment really resonated with me. In my mind, it translated to "Just because you can do something doesn't mean that you should." Sure, there are a number of things that Carla Harris can do, and do quite well, but just because I can doesn't mean that I should. I realized that if I wanted to be a powerful leader, then I should empower others, as many others as possible, so I could be out from under some of the execution to be free to evolve into a leader who could spend their time motivating and inspiring others to produce and achieve beyond that which they thought they could do. I wanted to evolve into that leader who could see opportunity amidst chaos or transform a culture while in a tumultuous context.

Every now and then, I enjoy watching a baseball game. And another thing that helped to move me along on my leadership journey was a little baseball imagery. I thought to myself, "Carla Harris, the terrific capital markets banker who executed deals that generated millions of dollars of revenue for the firm, was standing on first base. But Carla, the visionary leader who could create three great products from a blank sheet of paper. Products that could be a part of our firm's future growth strategy. Now the leader who could find opportunity amidst chaos or transform a culture in a tumultuous environment is standing on second base. Well, Carla," I said to myself, "you can't get to second base with your foot still on first; you must be willing to let go." That was powerful imagery for me, which helped me to keep moving forward in my journey to be a strong leader.

DIVERSITY

I find it interesting that we are roughly thirty years into the corporate conversation about diversity. It was around 1990 when companies first started to talk openly about the need to have a more diverse workforce. The context of the conversation was a sense of fairness. It was considered "the right thing to do." Initially, the conversation centered around people of color, most often African Americans. There was clear, indisputable evidence that people of color could hold successful leadership positions in corporate and civic America. We saw very successful Black mayors and executives at Xerox, IBM, and other large corporations. But there was widespread talk about the need for more diversity in the lower ranks of corporations as well as at the top of more organizations, and for diversity training and programs. By the end of the decade, the context of diversity conversations started to include women and to focus on having more of them in positions of power and authority in corporate organizations in general. And five years later, it also started to include members of the LGBTQ community. But I wonder, if we have been having this conversation for over thirty years, why don't we have more success? What went wrong?

Interestingly enough, while the original conversation around diversity emanated from the thesis that it was the right thing to do, it is that very perspective that has been one of the two main impediments to progress in corporate diversity. My argument is that while people might have different definitions of "the right thing to do," largely based on who they are, where they are from, and how they were raised, most business people generally tend to agree on what is commercial, strategic, or beneficial in a corporate context.

If diversity had always been viewed through the lens of a commercial imperative or of strategic importance to a company's competitive survival or as a critical component to profitability, then I believe the world would have made much more progress in the last thirty years.

We would have more women and people of color in positions of leadership and authority, greater equity in compensation and opportunity, and more diversity among the rank and file. If you think about it, there is no piece of a corporation's strategy that is thirty years in the making if it is seen as essential to a corporation's competitive survival or critical to a CEO's ability to drive shareholder value and therefore keep his or her seat!

If the perspective or lens has been one of the impediments to progress, then the other has been fear. Fear of litigation, fear that some group of people in the organization will lose if another group wins, fear that focusing on diversity will not yield better performance results, fear of deploying the wrong strategy, fear of backlash by white employees, fear of saying the wrong thing, or fear that if you say the wrong thing, then you may look as if you are out of touch or just don't have a clue! I could go on and on with the various fears that have impeded progress in the diversity journey. This fear turns into an impediment that thwarts progress and forward motion. It causes leaders to ignore the need for change or at best to make small, ineffective changes, or in other words, to tread water and go nowhere.

A couple of years ago, I gave a talk about some of the "pearls" from my first book, *Expect to Win*, at the headquarters of a Fortune 500 company. Afterward, the organizers invited me to spend time with the CEO and his twenty-plus direct reports. In this closed leadership session, the CEO asked me directly, "Carla, we can't seem to find or keep senior people of color. When we find one and bring them into the organization, they stay for two or three years and then they leave because they were not the right fit. We are trying, but what are we supposed to do?" He went on to add, "I do not know what to say to people who just do not embrace the fact that we have to take some action to have more diversity within our leadership ranks and within our organization for our long-term success."

As I considered how to answer this second question, I thought to myself, "Here is where more data would be helpful. Perhaps if we could show irrefutable data on the positive impacts of diversity, equity, and inclusion to those people who do not yet embrace DEI strategies as a value add to the company, then perhaps they would be faster to comply rather than create arguments, obstacles, and impediments to successfully integrating the strategies." Fast-forward to a few years later, and the data now exists. More and more data is constantly being released into the marketplace as shareholders start to increasingly think about DEI as a part of the environmental, social, and governance (ESG) lens they use to evaluate and invest in company stocks. I realized that I needed to give him an answer to help his employees understand his "why?" for diversity. As the CEO, he believed that DEI would drive his company's operational performance and therefore his success as a leader.

As a leader, you generally want to build consensus around any strategy you introduce. You want it to be embraced and executed by your best leaders and the employees who report to them. While the "my way or the highway" leadership style might have prevailed in the 1980s, 1990s, and early 2000s, as Millennials and Gen Zers entered the workforce, they began to challenge leaders on workplace directives.

I like to joke that, in those decades when Boomers were still the dominant population in the workforce, if the boss said, "Jump," Boomers asked, "How high?" Today, when the boss says, "Jump," Millennials ask, "Why?" As a leader, you must be sure to present your organization's DEI strategies as an integral part of the operational strategy, clearly demonstrating its value add to the organization as well as the penalty if it is not effectively implemented. It is important that you get the organization to understand that focusing on DEI is not a zero-sum game where someone must lose in order for someone else to win. Rather, as a leader, you must educate and sell others, especially your leaders, on the fact that there is a strategic and competitive benefit to making DEI your culture's default instead of an "add-on." EVERYONE stands to gain if you are successful.

I paused for a moment to carefully answer his first question now. I asked, "How many interviews do candidates for senior positions participate in before receiving an offer?" He explained, "It is easily fifteen to eighteen interviews, usually involving every member of the C-suite, the leaders of all our major businesses, and a few others." I said, "Wow. Eighteen interviews, huh? You *all* have to give a thumbs-up before a candidate gets the offer. So that means if they are hired and then shortly afterward decide to leave, you *all* made a recruiting mistake?"

He was stunned but immediately got my point. I went on to say, "If a candidate does not make it here after going through eighteen interviews before they are hired, I cannot believe that you *all* made a recruiting mistake. Something is obviously happening once the candidate comes on board. There is something within the culture that is prompting these candidates to make the decision to leave. Sounds like you might want to check inside."

I'm glad to report that he took my advice. He commissioned the CHRO to conduct a confidential survey to ascertain the views of people within the organization, especially people of color. The survey uncovered employee perspectives about lack of access to roles, compensation, promotions, and the like, that were starkly negative and suggested that the organization was in peril of losing more talent, especially talent of color.

LEADERSHIP GEM:

Today's employees are looking for representation in their leaders. They want to see people who look like them with a seat at the table.

When today's talent assesses a potential company to work for, one of their top priorities is representation, particularly in the senior levels. They want to work for organizations where they can see themselves. To show the kind of representation your organization needs to attract new and diverse talent, you will have to engage in lateral recruiting.

While every company would love to bring people in at the entry level and grow and develop them to be senior executives, we do not have that luxury in our current environment. It takes at least ten years to grow and develop a senior executive, yet the rate of innovation is almost a tenth of that time, twelve to eighteen months—you cannot wait for someone to mature enough to lead and still compete in the marketplace. In addition, over the course of ten years, you will have at least two bear market cycles, during which you might endure a couple of reductions in force and therefore lose some of the women and/or people of color in your pipeline that you recruited and have been trying to develop.

Here is where lateral recruiting is so important. You can hire people away from competitors or other industries to fill in some of the roles where you lack representation. However, if you are going to engage in lateral recruiting, you must be careful of organ rejection. You might wonder how organ rejection relates to hiring people. Consider this analogy. If you have ever known anyone who has had a successful kidney or liver transplant, then you know that the surgeons will usually prescribe at least twenty drugs following the surgery. These drugs support the body in holding on to the new organ. The reason? Despite the fact that the body needs the kidney or liver, it will naturally dispel that which is foreign. It is the same for people you hire laterally. As the leader, you will need to overinvest in their success and integration and ensure that they feel included in order to heighten the probability that they will be absorbed into the organization, be embraced by the culture and other senior executives, and stay with your team.

Why Should You Care About Diversity?

Until recently, as we discussed, the answer to the question "Why care about diversity?" has been largely driven by the general consensus that it was the right thing to do. But enough data now exists to credibly move the diversity conversation from being the right thing to do to being the commercially smart thing to do. Recent studies, many conducted by leading management consulting firms (such as McKinsey & Company's 2020 report *Diversity Wins: How Inclusion Matters*), have revealed hard, commercial data and solid research that show having more women, for example, on boards and in senior management positions leads to less stock price volatility, better return on equity, and better overall performance.

LEADERSHIP GEM:

Good leaders understand that diversity is good for teams and good for business.

As a leader, you will be tasked with increasing profitability, market share, stock price, and customer penetration, and diversity is going to be an increasingly larger component of your success equation. As the talent pool, particularly in the United States, becomes more and more diverse, your ability to be successful as a leader will depend on your ability to attract and retain this diverse talent to drive innovation and success in your organization. While boards of directors and shareholders will certainly continue to value a CEO's ability to create the right operational strategy for the company to drive shareholder value, they will increasingly place a greater value on the human capital strategy and the CEO's ability to build and retain diverse teams, both at the top of the organization and throughout the employee pipeline.

In 2016, I started presenting a business case for diversity in some of my speeches and conversations with corporate thought leaders because I kept hearing decision makers speaking about diversity as being the right thing to do. I implore all leaders to be intentional in their dogged pursuit of understanding how diversity can and should be integral to your strategy and revenue creation, and why it is a business driver for your company.

We've established the importance of innovation to be competitive across all industries today. If you need one innovative idea to obtain and retain a leadership position, internally or externally, then it follows that you will need many more ideas in the room where they are developed—that is where innovation is born. To have a lot of ideas in the room, you better have a lot of perspectives in the room, because ideas are born from perspectives. If you need a lot of perspectives in the room, you need to have a lot of experiences in the room because perspectives are born from experiences. Finally, if you need a lot of experiences in the room, you must begin with a lot of different kinds of people in the room because experiences are born from people. Thus, to arrive at the one innovative idea that will allow your team and company to lead, you have to start with a lot of different kinds of people in the room. This is the business case for diversity.

LEADERSHIP GEM:

There is no innovation without diversity.

If driving innovation isn't enough to convince you as a leader that diversity is something you should focus on, consider this argument. When I walked out of Harvard Business School over thirty years ago, excellence in corporate America looked like six white men at the top. Pick any company—IBM, Goldman Sachs, Ford, GM, Morgan Stanley, Procter and Gamble—six white men were at the top. The CEO, CFO, COO, CIO, CHRO, and CMO, that was the norm. As a result, I knew that if I wanted to "play" in this corporate sandbox, then I would have to be very comfortable being "the first" and "the only" in most rooms. Frankly, the notion of being the first or the only was not daunting at all to me because that's the way things were at the time. By the time I finished high school, I'd already had so many experiences like that.

However, this is not the environment that Millennials and Gen Zers have grown up in. They have grown up in an environment where they see women lead. They may even have a mother who is in the C-suite or at the helm of a very-high-profile nonprofit. They went to diverse schools, where there is a smart Black kid sitting to their right, a smart LatinX kid sitting to their left, a smart Asian kid sitting in front of them, and a smart Indian kid sitting behind them. To them, this is what excellence looks like, and if they do not see their definition of excellence reflected in the organizations they are considering joining, they will not join. In addition, if they do join, they will not stay for any length of time, threatening any company's objective to be the employer of choice in their industry.

If you are not yet convinced of the "why," let me offer you another compelling argument. It used to be that corporations served three primary constituents: shareholders, customers, and employees. Each of these constituents had a powerful tool. If the shareholders did not agree with something about the company or its leader, they could sell their stock. If the customers did not like something about the company, they could refuse to buy the organization's products or services. If employees did not like something about the company, they could always quit.

Today, corporations have a fourth constituent . . . community. Community is not local, it is global, and it also has a powerful tool, called social media. If a corporation takes an action that community does not like or agree with, or the leader acts in a way that offends the global community, then in only seconds, the company can suffer massive brand degradation or lose billions of dollars of market capitalization as the distaste goes viral.

Diversity has become one of the barometers of value that these four constituents really care about. Boards of directors are asking about it in the boardroom, consumers are reading company annual reports or DEI initiative reports, and the global community is constantly trolling social media to learn how the companies whose products they use and support feel about and act upon diversity.

Allyship

As companies have advanced on their DEI journeys over the last five years, the words *ally* and *allyship* have come into focus. These terms became popular in mid-to-late 2020 as leaders struggled to navigate the environment of social unrest and their employees' demand for a corporate response. Leaders felt pressure to assess their role in helping to advance the causes and concerns of the multicultural professionals who reported to them, and they worked to understand these professionals' corporate experiences and what they could do to improve their organizational standing.

The Dictionary.com definition of *ally* as a noun is a person who "aligns with and supports a cause with another individual or group of people." While I agree with this definition, the real question—a good one, which I received a lot in 2020—is "What does it mean to be a good ally?," or, even better, "What should a good ally *do*?"

My response was that a good ally should "listen, act, and repeat." Allyship is about both presence and voice. It is about showing up and being present in rooms where those who do not have a voice, or an equal voice, in the organization are not in attendance or do not have access. It is also about exercising *your* voice on their behalf when you are in those rooms. But to be a good ally, you must first be able to identify with that person or group, and to do that you have to LISTEN to their experience, their voice, and understand their point of view in order to get a new perspective, often one that may be very different from what you thought to be true. Not only is it important to listen, but you must also be open to what you hear.

Kamora was asked to present an update to the company's president on her team's DEI awareness program. She and some of her colleagues had been tasked with implementing training and exercises designed to help create a more inclusive environment on the team. During the presentation, Kamora shared some of the results of the DEI program, but also added that she was struggling with her supervisor's lack of support for the program, and that he often made statements and used language that was gender-biased, disrespectful, and dismissive to her and the other women on the team. Rather than accepting Kamora's experience as true for her and perhaps looking to help provide a way forward, the president labeled Kamora's presentation as negative. He had worked with the supervisor for years and immediately decided that Kamora must be imagining or misunderstanding the supervisor's comments. But to be an ally, you must be willing to challenge your idea of what you think is true and be open to the experiences and reality of others.

Once you have listened, understood your employee's perspective, and considered what is transpiring in the organization, why it might be happening, and how it could be creating inequity, then it is time to act. Your presence and power give you access to people, rooms, and conversations that allow you to make a difference as an ally. When you are in the room, you can use your power to make a decision to act on someone's behalf. Further, you can ask THE question that makes everyone in the room hear the bias or discrimination in a discussion, or that raises awareness of the inequity in how decisions are being made, as well as how they could be improved.

There was an opening to lead a marketing strategy for one of a company's most important products. Daniel recommended Soneil for the position: Soneil had been at the company for eight years, and during his tenure he had been assigned a few low-profile products, all of which were struggling when he assumed responsibility. But under his leadership, they were successfully transformed into more productive assets for the company. In a meeting of the executive vice presidents, Margaret suggested Eric, who had been at the company for only three years, for the role; Eric had been assigned as the lead product manager for two very-high-profile products. When Daniel presented Soneil's candidacy, Margaret and a couple of other EVPs argued that Soneil didn't really have the "presence" needed for this very public-facing role. They felt the candidate for this assignment needed "gravitas" in the marketplace and that Eric was "much better suited." John, another EVP who had been at the company for a while and was expected to be the successor to the president, asked, "Margaret, when you say Soneil doesn't have presence, what do you mean? Why don't you think that he has gravitas in the market, given what he has done to turn around some very tough brands?" Furthermore, "What is it about Eric that gives him that gravitas, or why do you think that he is a better candidate for this opportunity?" Margaret could not give an answer that was beyond her personal opinion or feelings, and ultimately Soneil received the assignment.

In this case, John acted as an ally for Soneil by simply asking questions that pushed the conversation beyond what was typical, or an acceptance of Margaret's point of view. By doing so he arrested a process that would have resulted in an outcome based on a perception or a feeling versus facts. To be an ally means taking the time and making the effort to question the status quo, to be sure that everyone has equal access to opportunities based on their accomplishments and qualifications.

What Does It Take to Implement a Successful DEI Program?

As I've said before, whenever I hear senior leaders talking about diversity and using phrases like "it is hard," "it is difficult to find . . . ," "it will not happen quickly," I generally conclude that they are not serious about making changes in their organization or they don't really believe that diversity, equity, and inclusion (DEI) are critical to the organization's operational success and competitive performance.

As a leader, if you start with the perspective that something is going to be difficult or is impossible, then you will encounter unnecessary difficulties and may ultimately block your own success. Honestly, developing and implementing a long-term, competitive, and sustainable DEI program is not that difficult. In fact, you can see real changes in the organization in as soon as one calendar year. To have a successful diversity effort, you need three things: intentionality, accountability, and consistency.

Intentionality

Diversity will not just happen. You must be intentional about it and focus on it. When you are hiring new people, you must be intentional about making directives to your recruiters, executive and internal, to make sure that you and your hiring managers are seeing a wide range of diverse candidates. You must be explicit about making sure you have an opportunity to see *all* the talent available in the market that fits the specific job requirements, because talent does not come from only one demographic. Your recruiters and hiring managers must understand that their job is to find talent from all demographics, and as a leader you must hold them accountable for that.

LEADERSHIP GEM:

Great leaders accept that we all have biases and look for ways to mitigate them in hiring, development, and elsewhere.

Intentionality is critical because we all have unconscious bias, and it particularly hides within the processes, procedures, and cultures of most organizations. Bias is created in how you were raised, where you are from, how you are educated, and how you have been treated in your previous experiences and by whom. You will often hear me say, "Bias is sneaky; you don't realize when it has invaded your thought process and thus your decision-making." It is particularly exacerbated if you have many people from the same demographic (race, gender, education, geographic, and/or experiential backgrounds), where bias is more likely to increase and become ingrained as a part of the culture.

For example, consider the financial services industry back in the 1980s and 1990s. The top-tier investment banks all recruited from the same Ivy League schools (Harvard, Yale, Princeton, Brown, Columbia, U Penn, Cornell, and Dartmouth). Most of the available spots for the incoming class of analysts could easily be filled by candidates from those schools. Further, candidates from those schools were more likely to get an opportunity for a first-round interview because the people reviewing the résumés were alumni from those schools. They knew the schools' curriculums, which of the majors were challenging, what on-campus jobs and activities were important, etc. If a résumé from an unfamiliar school made it into the pile, it would not be reviewed through the same lens and, save some extenuating circumstance, would not likely be competitive and considered for a first-round interview. This is the definition of bias.

In most environments, bias exists when the people making decisions about who should be on a team, who is on the short list for a promotion, who will run a department, who will speak to the board—and I could go on—come from a similar demographic. In most cases, they will choose the person who is most like them. Until recently, individuals in corporate America were unaware of how prevalent bias is in most cultures and therefore were not intentional about creating policies, procedures, and processes that would avoid it. Even today, unconscious bias training is still optional for many decision makers.

I have to admit, I would have said that as a self-aware, highly educated woman of color, I was very aware of my own biases and did not think I had *any* unconscious bias, until I had an incident where it was on full display. I mentioned creating the Multicultural Innovation Lab at Morgan Stanley. It is an in-house accelerator for tech-enabled companies that have been founded by entrepreneurs of color and women. When these companies are accepted into the Lab, they receive capital in exchange for a small ownership percentage in their business; content specifically designed to help them evolve from being a founder to a

CEO; and connections to some of our investment banking clients to help accelerate the scaling of their businesses. Eighteen months after starting the endeavor, I looked up and my entire team was women. Not an ounce of testosterone to be seen anywhere! I knew immediately that I had a gap in my go to market strategy because I was missing an important voice at the table.

If you have homogenous thinking at your decision-making table, you will have a gap in your go to market strategy and it will expose you to outsize competitive threats. As a result of this revelation, I became intentional about making sure that our next two hires in the Lab were men. We have numerous recent examples of companies that had homogenous thinking at the decision-making table and ended up with great challenges in the market. One company released an ad that the public thought was offensive and which cost the company some brand value. They had no diversity at the table when the decision was made. When you are operating in an intense, dynamic, fast-paced environment, it is easy to reach for the familiar; we all do it. If you are going to be a powerful leader, however, you must push against this tendency, particularly if it is a highly competitive environment.

LEADERSHIP GEM:

When you are in a fast-paced environment, it is easy to reach for people who are like you. Intentional leaders will develop the discipline to reach first for people who are different from them in some way—race, gender, educational or geographical background.

If you do not have a diverse leadership team, then you must be intentional about changing it. Why? Because today's new workers are looking for representation in leadership. As we've discussed, Millennials and Gen Zers have to "see it in order to believe it." They are not apt to believe that diversity will come to the organization after they arrive. They will more likely think the organization does not care about diversity and the organization is not a place where they are likely to do well. As a result, they either will look for employment elsewhere or will join with a high degree of skepticism and leave as soon as something goes awry, negatively impacting the organization's retention statistics.

Intentionally creating diversity in your organization is not difficult, nor do you have to change any requirements or lower standards. I have heard various leaders say, "We want to have diversity on the team (or department or at the leadership level), but we don't want to lower our standards, or promote someone just because they are a woman or a person of color." Those kinds of statements typically mean that person sees diversity as a "nice to have" rather than a value add; or they are unaware of their unconscious bias and will not likely help the organization drive transformation and innovation; or they are attempting to use fear as a tactic to sway other key decision makers to be skeptical about adding diverse people to the leadership ranks.

I quickly respond to people who state that diversity programs equate with lowering standards, saying, "Be careful of using that kind of fear-based language to scare people about bringing in diverse talent. If there is one thing I know for sure, it is that no woman or person of color would ever want you to lower the bar to bring them into the organization. That would be a direct insult to the hard work they've invested in their careers." In most cases, this statement stops the conversation from continuing in this direction and we can then proceed with more constructive and creative thoughts.

LEADERSHIP GEM:

As a leader, you must make sure your team understands that diverse means different, not less qualified.

My experience has been that creating diversity in an organization, particularly in the leadership ranks, is relatively simple. A senior leader once told me, "Carla, my executive operating committee is relatively new and most of them are white men. There won't be a seat available for a woman or a person of color for at least five years. What am I to do in the meantime?"

My answer? "Add a seat."

If there was not a rule or specific reason the committee was limited to six seats, then why couldn't he make it seven? To me, creating more diversity is just that simple. This organization was experiencing a decline in its retention numbers, particularly among younger employees. The company's employee survey indicated that the lack of diversity in the organization was a big source of discontent and it was having an increasingly difficult time recruiting women and people of color, particularly at middle and senior levels. Why was adding a seat so difficult, particularly when there were easily a dozen candidates with outstanding company experience, stellar educational pedigrees, and demonstrated leadership skills?

To be a powerful, intentional leader, you have to focus on who you are hiring, and on the process for identifying talent and placing people in visible positions of leadership and authority. It won't happen on its own because of the aforementioned unconscious bias. Further, it is human nature to continue doing what has always been done, particularly if there is no pressure to do things differently. Even when a directive exists, if leaders, hiring managers, and others are not made accountable, they are not apt to change their behavior. Especially if they do not really see the value of doing it differently or feel that the current process is wrong.

Accountability

Accountability is required for anything to change. Over the course of the thirty-year discussion about diversity, I have seen many companies create programs, policies, guidelines, and goals, but without a measure of accountability for achieving these goals, long-term, sustainable success was impossible. For diversity programs and initiatives to be successful, they require three important components of accountability.

First, there must be a clear demonstration of commitment from the top. The CEO, chair, or president must clearly articulate the organization's commitment to diversity, supported by what the company has done, is doing, or intends to do to demonstrate this commitment. The integral role the diversity program plays in the organization's strategy and its ability to compete must be made clear, as well as an intention to monitor it and hold leaders accountable. This first step is vital. The message must come from the top for any DEI efforts to have credibility in any company. The CEO should also appoint diverse people within the organization to high-profile roles; be personally involved in recruiting respected, diverse industry talent; and engage in town halls or other programs with women and people of color. And the CEO's words and actions must be synergistic and reinforcing.

Second, there *must* be a method for holding leaders accountable to DEI goals and objectives. I have seen many companies set targets and objectives and ask leaders to set individual goals and objectives, yet if the goals are not achieved, there is no measure of accountability through compensation, promotion, or other assignments. In most organizations, people behave according to how they are rewarded. For example, if driving revenue is important, that is, will result in handsome remuneration or promotions, which also result in higher compensation, then all objectives other than revenue generation are considered tertiary. If keeping costs down or contained is the metric of success, then behaviors that contain costs will be rewarded. When it comes to diversity, while goals may be established, there are often no measures of accountability or even conversations about it when the time comes to evaluate or assess a leader's success.

LEADERSHIP GEM:

Successful leaders understand that what gets measured gets done. The most successful DEI programs have accountability built in.

If DEI is truly going to be an organization's strategic imperative, then it has to be treated like all other strategic and operational imperatives. In a leader's annual performance review, if DEI strategies are integrated into the operations of the company, how that leader leverages and develops talent must be part of the discussion. Just as a C-suite leader is evaluated on their ability to attain revenue, profitability, and market share growth, maintain cost objectives, implement strategy, and interact with the board, evaluators must also assess the leader's level of success with their human capital strategy. Key considerations should be: How diverse is the leader's team? Does the succession pipeline include diverse candidates for key roles? What is the percentage of diverse candidates hired relative to the total hires? What are the demographics of the leader's direct reports? Has the leader engaged in leadership development in the last year? If there is equal time and consideration given to human capital management (HCM), of which DEI is a key part, then leaders get the message that it *truly matters* to the organization in the same way that other strategic parameters matter to the organization. When other professionals know their performance related to DEI will impact their opportunities and pockets, they will execute with the same intention they place on other strategic objectives.

Some companies have implemented specific diversity awards for people who are executing DEI objectives well, particularly related to hiring. While this methodology can be effective, it is often focused on numbers or how many diverse bodies are brought into the organization. What's missing is a process to truly assess whether the candidates are top-caliber, long-term players. If these candidates don't bring the requisite skills and expertise to their roles, they typically leave after a very short period of time, unable to meet the company's performance standards. Unfortunately, organizations that do not embrace the benefits of diversity may point to these candidates as examples of the inefficacy of DEI efforts. The reality is, these people were not great hires. It has nothing to do with their diversity, but rather everything to do with the people who pushed them through the process merely to realize incentives rather than hiring candidates who are diverse *and* highly qualified.

When DEI strategies are handled properly, as a part of a leader's evaluative process and clearly as much a part of the overall reward as other key metrics, then the strategies have a much higher probability of long-term success. It must be clear that HCM, of which DEI strategies are an integral part, are as important as revenue targets and can be measured by qualified bodies and the retention of those bodies—how employees move through the organization, the feedback they receive, and the impact they have on the organization. Then leaders will find ways to deliver outstanding DEI results, just as they do for other important metrics.

While the C-suite leader's demonstrated commitment is important, it is not the only key to developing and sustaining a successful DEI effort. Many efforts are often sabotaged and die in what I like to call the "immovable middle." Middle-level managers are often the people who confound DEI strategies and present barriers to women and people of color moving up in an organization. This results in great women and candidates of color leaving. Many of these managers hold their positions not because they are great people leaders but because they are great producers. They may not embrace diversity as an important part of the operational strategy and often feel that by supporting or promoting diverse candidates, they may lose opportunities themselves. These managers can become obstacles, particularly in environments where there are no accountability measures in place for the DEI strategy.

When a great diverse candidate leaves, the middle manager creates a false narrative about their departure to cover up the loss. By the time the CEO hears that the candidate is no longer with the organization, the narrative is far different from the reality. Accountability for DEI is particularly important at the middle-manager level, and it must be consistent across all economic cycles and leadership changes.

Consistency

People often ask me, "Why haven't we seen more success with respect to diverse candidates working on or in senior positions on Wall Street?" My answer is consistent: Diversity in financial services has largely been a bull market phenomenon. When there is a bull market and things are going well, substantial resources are allocated to DEI in the form of increased hiring and programs, focus on succession pipelines, etc. However, in bear markets, when the stock market declines and we have interest rate volatility, reductions in force, corporate restructurings, etc., the focus on diversity declines as well.

It doesn't necessarily completely go away, but the intensity level drops from a 10 to a 2 at best. Plus, in times of restructurings and lay-offs, small populations like women and people of color are typically disproportionately impacted. By the time we emerge from the bear market and start heading to a better economy, the pipeline that you worked so hard to build has been virtually wiped out.

To have long-term success with any DEI program, maintaining a consistent level of investment throughout all economic cycles is critical. Otherwise, you expose yourself to the "boom and bust" phenomenon that we have seen in the financial services industry over the last thirty years. If you get into this cycle, you compromise your ability to get your entire organization on board and committed to the DEI strategy. Employees who are excited and enthusiastic about the strategy and committed to its success will start to lose interest, assuming your lack of consistency means DEI is not really important to the company.

Those cynical employees will now feel even more strongly that the strategy is not something they need to pay attention to, also compromising your success.

If you stay committed to consistency even in down cycles, then you can be a net beneficiary as an employer. In fact, during downturns, you should be even more aggressive about engaging in lateral recruiting efforts, especially of diverse candidates. During downturns, many employees become unsettled and start to reflect on their experiences, rethinking their careers with their current employers. As a leader who is looking for great talent, you might find some of your competitors in a vulnerable, unsettled state because of the economic environment and be able to recruit their employees into your organization.

Consistency in your DEI efforts enhances your company's reputation and reinforces the perception that the company is a leader in HCM and is truly committed to its DEI strategy, striving to create an environment where all kinds of talent has an opportunity to outperform and thrive.

INNOVATION

We've talked a lot about innovation and its direct connection to competition. Every company in every industry you can think of is racing not only to compete to survive but to be the first, to be the best, to drive customer behavior and adoption, and they have to innovate to do it. As we discussed in the previous section, diverse teams are the key to successful, sustainable innovation. Homogeneous teams produce homogenous thinking and will expose a gap in a company's go to market strategy.

How do companies teach their employees to be innovative, to take risks, to do that which has never been done before? The answer is to teach them how to fail. In order to repeatedly take the risk to try new things, teams must be comfortable with failing. The easiest way to get team members comfortable with failure is to celebrate them.

I am not suggesting that you and your team make a habit of constantly failing. What I am saying is that when a member takes a risk and tries something new on behalf of the team and it does not work out, it is your job as the leader to applaud them for taking the risk in the first place. Acknowledge the failure and then actually or figuratively clap for the employee or the team for making the attempt.

The one thing you cannot do is to negatively overreact to the failure itself. If you make a big deal when someone on your team tries something new and the outcome is not successful, or you publicly admonish them or, worse, ridicule them, what you do is stifle the risk appetite of other members of your team. The result will be the opposite of what you want to happen. Going forward, no one will dare try anything new for fear of your public retribution. Soon your team will be stuck, stifled, and will lose its competitiveness internally and in the broader marketplace.

Teaching your team how to fail also means that sometimes you, as the leader, have to push them to work on the edge. In fact, in some cases you'll have to push them until they fail. You must continue to ask questions and challenge them to go further until you have exhausted all possible outcomes.

Vic was the head trader for a large investment bank and managed five young traders. He was constantly telling them that they needed to develop a muscle for taking calculated risks. He coached them to watch particular stocks and their momentum in the market. He taught them to notice how others were buying and selling, in what quantities, and at what prices. He helped them develop judgment, taking into account the news of the day and opinions around how the stock would or would not react to news, and then use that judgment to make a bet on a trade.

One day, Steve, one of the brightest young traders on Vic's team, saw a lot of volume in a particular stock. There was news in the industry that day and Steve made a large bet to short the stock, thinking that it would react negatively to the news and make him a huge profit. Unfortunately, the news that was reported actually caused the stock to go up relative to the price at which Steve had shorted it. In the end, he lost a lot of money for the desk.

Vic blew a gasket! He chewed Steve out, yelling and screaming at him, complete with name-calling and expletives right on the trading floor in front of everyone. Steve was devasted, defeated, and embarrassed. The other young traders on the team were shocked and upset, many thinking to themselves, "I'll never make an outsize bet like that on my own." From then on, Vic made the rule that all trades had to be signed off on and cleared by him. While Vic's objective was to have the young traders learn how to think for themselves, develop a nose for taking risks, innovate, and trade on their own, he blocked that from happening by attacking Steve for his mistake, thus failing as a leader and a developer of talent.

INCLUSIVENESS

C-suite executives often ask me, "What does it mean to show up as an inclusive leader? How does inclusivity manifest itself in leadership?"

The answer is simple. Solicit people's voices.

Try the following exercise. The next time your team comes together to discuss, for example, a new go to market strategy for a product, you might say, "By the end of our meeting, we want to have a solution and a strategy to go to market with this product. I'd like to see us determine the how, when, and where of the strategy and develop a concrete plan of action. I will start with a strawman. Then I'd like to hear from each of you. Do you agree with the strategy or not? How might we improve it? Where do you see potential gaps?"

After you have articulated a strawman idea, to get the ball rolling, choose a team member who is comfortable offering their ideas. Say something like "Okay, Nancy. How would you add to this idea? How do we make it better?" Then add, "Okay, those are great ideas. Howard, how would you refute this strategy? Let's play devil's advocate; why wouldn't this work? What are the risks?"

Then include others by bringing them into the conversation, "Pam, what are other reasons why this might not work? Taylor, what are the anecdotes to this issue? How would we fix these things?"

By using this approach, you are helping your team develop their collaboration muscles. More specifically, how not to be defensive when a fellow team member challenges their ideas. As a leader, you are fostering a greater sense of cohesiveness on the team, teaching them to all work together on a solution as well as to work side by side with YOU!

More important, you are demonstrating inclusiveness. By actively asking each one of them for their ideas and to make a contribution, you are implicitly saying, "I see you," to each one of them. In your response to each one of their ideas, you are effectively saying, "I hear you." Everyone, no matter who they are, values being seen and heard, especially by a leader. I guarantee that no matter what you are trying to accomplish, if you use this strategy with your team, each member will feel valued and included in the process.

LEADERSHIP GEM:

People value being seen, and as a leader, you have an opportunity to inspire people when you recognize them. It is a way of saying, "You are important to this team; I value that you are here." It is extremely empowering.

Another important consequence of this exercise? Engage in it the next four times you gather your team, and when you gather them for a fifth meeting, you won't have to make the effort to solicit their voices and ideas; you will see that they will come to the meeting ready to contribute. They will rise to your level of expectations, but they will also meet the challenge of whatever task or project that is before them. Ultimately, you want everyone's imprimatur on the blueprint for a project. When everyone's fingerprints are on the blueprint to complete a project, then each of your team members is invested in its success or failure.

Having a strategy to ensure inclusion is essential if you want the investment of finding and retaining diverse talent to yield any results. If people don't feel that they are a part of an organization, that their voice and contribution are valued, then they will deliver the requirements of the job description, at best. In most cases this is probably well below what they have the capacity to deliver. A common saying in DEI circles is "Diversity is being invited to the party, and inclusion is being asked to dance." As a leader, it is critical that you develop a strategy to make sure that people feel they are an integral part of the culture, that the company's success depends upon their contribution. This is especially important when you are bringing diverse talent into the organization and they are one of a few relative to the large organization. Just because you hired them doesn't mean they will feel comfortable and included. When any of us feel uncomfortable in any situation, it compromises what we can produce.

Amidst the turmoil of the social unrest in 2020, I had a conversation with a leader. He asked, "Carla, how do you know that you have arrived, that you have been successful with your DEI strategy?" I told him, "You know you have made progress when you have traveled from diversity to inclusion, to equity, and finally to belonging. BELONGING is the holy grail. When you hear your people throughout the organization saying things like 'my CEO, my manager, my colleagues, my company.' When they are talking about their career and the company and using possessive nouns almost unconsciously, then you have made progress. Even then, you won't be done. You will have to continue to evolve as your workforce and your operational strategy change, but you will be well on the journey to having a productive culture."

VOICE

One of the most important hallmarks of a powerful leader is to have the courage to exercise your voice. In the speeches I give to organizations around the world, I have become known for saying, "You have to be willing to call a thing a thing." It is easy for us to abdicate the use of our voice, especially around emotionally sensitive topics or about subjects that might be deemed to be hot politically or unpopular in your environment. And the truth is we have all done it.

However, the price of wearing the leadership jersey is having the courage to speak up not only during the normal course of business but especially when you see something happening that is wrong. Your team members and others who are directly or even indirectly reporting to you are looking to you for guidance. They are watching to see how you handle situations, how you receive and accept the inevitable changes that take place within an organization, or how you express your feelings about a restructuring, reduction in force, buyout of another company, or other events that take place. Your team members are going to look to you and how you behave as an example of how they should respond.

Here is an example of a leader who could have used her voice to create a different outcome. Aris had been the CEO of a top company for ten years. But the company was going through a tough time. Competitors were ramping up their marketing spend, introducing new products at a rapid pace, and shifting consumers' tastes. The company was also laboring under an unprecedented amount of debt and, as a result, had dramatically downsized its workforce and was under intense pressure from activist shareholders to make even more changes.

Aris called the entire workforce together for a global, company-wide meeting. She believed the only way for the company to regain its former standing was for all employees to pull together and try to understand, embrace, and move forward with the company's new strategy. However, most of the officers, employees, and rank and file had no motivation to do any of that. They were demoralized, tired, and beginning to question the company's strategy. The prevailing doubt, the cafeteria and watercooler talk, was whether the company would ever regain its top position in the marketplace.

During the meeting, rather than focus her remarks on acknowledging how people really felt, Aris instead chose to focus on the competitive marketplace, the strategy, and the way forward. As a result, the employees left the meeting knowing more about the strategy, but with continued ambivalence about their commitment to strapping in and dedicating themselves to helping the company reclaim its number one position. Shortly afterward, the company's key executives, rising stars, and emerging leaders started to jump ship, taking jobs with competitors. Subsequently, the company continued to lose ground to the competition and has yet to regain its leadership status in the industry.

This is an instance where the CEO should have leveraged her voice as a leader. She should have first acknowledged the reality of what employees were experiencing. Second, she should have acknowledged that she needed their help to right the ship and then ended with a charge to everyone, saying something like "I know this has been a tough period for us. We are used to being number one, not fighting for a place in the landscape. I know you have seen your colleagues, great colleagues, downsized, and they are no longer here. We believe we have completed the reductions in force needed to continue to compete and execute the extraordinary opportunity that we have at hand with this new strategy. I know you are tired. This has not been a fun period for me either. But I still believe in our company, our mission, and that we are the best in the industry. I believe that with your help, we will not just move forward, but we will move forward and regain our position as a market leader. I cannot do it alone. I need each of us to acknowledge our fatigue, our pain, and even our fear, and then embrace the way forward. We have seen a version of this movie before, and we have the power to create the ending. We have the best team in the industry, and together we can win. I am going to share a new strategy that we have developed, but I want your thoughts on how we can fill in any gaps and how we can best execute it. When we finish, I want every one of us to leave this meeting and go out and infect anyone who couldn't be here today with our new collective sense of optimism, and let's go WIN!"

In acknowledging what people were feeling, by giving VOICE to the elephant in the room, she would have taken the power away from that which was unspoken. By shining light on the grumblings and rumors, and calling out the cafeteria talk, and, even more important, by saying, "We are in this together," she would've shown that she felt the same way. She would have essentially said to the company's employees, "I see you."

As we have discussed, one of the most important things you can do as a leader is to indicate to the people you lead that you see them. Everyone values being *seen* and *heard*. Whenever there is an unspoken issue, the proverbial elephant in the room, left alone and unacknowledged, it only gets bigger. It grows and grows and eventually suffocates every great idea, people's willingness to coalesce, ultimately stifling any forward progress and success. The only way to stop it, to take its power away, is to call it out and acknowledge it.

To be clear, this is not about making a great speech. It is about the importance of acknowledging employees' feelings. It is about the importance of acknowledging that a prevailing negative attitude is a major challenge to any organization's ability to move forward and pursue a new and different strategy.

Aris's big challenge wasn't the lack of a plan; it was the team's inability to embrace and execute the plan because of what they were experiencing.

I observed another company in a similar position that adopted the strategy of giving voice to what they were experiencing. The employees rallied around the strategy *and* the leader, and the company eventually regained its leadership position in the industry. As a leader, using your voice also means holding the organization accountable to the virtues and strategies it has defined for itself and has articulated to the marketplace. For example, if an organization is committed to having a diverse workforce from top to bottom, then leadership should relentlessly focus on filling roles with senior women and people of color until it is apparent that there is a strong composition of different voices who are driving strong outcomes for the organization.

Further, leadership must continue to give voice to the fact that the organization is "behind," "not where it wants to be," and "working aggressively to make changes." Giving voice to an obvious deficit or issue will serve as a catalyst for more rapid change and will hold those recruiting and hiring accountable until the objective is met. The leadership cannot be satisfied with "trying" to fill the roles but instead must exhaust all internal and external sources for the talent and be committed to "the try" until the objective is achieved.

COURAGE

Courage is the strand that holds all the pearls of intentional leadership together. It takes courage to be your authentic self. It takes courage to engage enough with your people to listen to their ideas and what they have to say to build the trust you need to effectively lead them. It takes courage to create clarity for others when you cannot see what will happen down the road. And it takes courage to create other leaders and prepare them to take your seat, especially when you cannot clearly see the next step in your own career. Further, it takes courage to be intentional about diversity and to think about how to strategically incorporate it into any operational plan.

Many of today's corporate leaders, even those who consider themselves among the "disruptive" Silicon Valley CEOs, accept the status quo when it comes to hiring, developing, and retaining leaders. This is among the principal reasons that we are still talking about DEI in corporate America today. If leaders were courageous enough to create processes and procedures that would ensure they have consistent exposure to diverse talent, hiring practices that would eliminate unconscious bias, and intentional development and retention policies, then we would be much further along in terms of DEI and have far more multicultural and female senior leaders in corporations in this country and across the globe.

As I mentioned earlier in this book, the principal thing that makes leaders stall around DEI is fear. They fear that it is too hard to achieve success. They fear that things could go awry and the majority employees might resent it. They fear that it won't have the positive impact on financial results that it is purported to have; they fear that there could be an embarrassing headline. They fear that their leadership legacy will be tarnished if things don't work out well.

It takes courage to show up every day as an inclusive leader and, as we discussed in chapter 5, to make the extra effort to solicit other people's voices. It takes courage to try and fail, especially in highly technical environments where professionals are driven by facts and data and the black and white of an issue, and fear the retribution of being wrong.

It also takes courage to intentionally teach your teams how to fail. Yet, if a leader can create an environment where people are not afraid to do so, then the rate and quality of innovation would outpace that which we currently see in most environments.

LEADERSHIP GEM:

While it is not always easy or comfortable, direct communication and the courage to "call a thing a thing" are the fastest and most productive ways to a solution.

Last, it takes courage to "call a thing a thing," which is why so many leaders fail at this important pearl of leadership. It is far easier to talk around an issue or evade it altogether when the topic is hard or exposes clear gaps in a corporation's culture or leadership. Most leaders would rather talk about meritocracy than admit there cannot be a true meritocracy if there is a human element in the evaluative process. Even organizations that think they have meritocratic cultures and fair and objective evaluation processes often forget the human element of the process. Take an investment banking environment for an example. At the end of every year, young associates are judged primarily on how they have performed on quantitative and analytical assignments. However, there is a person who decides who gets which projects, which means all project assignments are not created equal. Then there are different people who judge the success of each assignment and who may each have different standards and expectations of performance. Therefore, they may each grade the same assignment differently. I could go on and on about the places where human assessments of "objective" work could ultimately impact the overall view of how an associate performed for the year.

The point is that in order to be a powerful, impactful, influential leader in today's environment, it takes courage to be intentional around the "gems" presented in this chapter. It takes courage to be intentionally vulnerable enough to connect with the people you work with, to show empathy, and to be authentic. If as a leader you can realize that courage is what you need in order to successfully execute with authenticity and clarity, ensuring diversity, inclusivity, and innovation, then you have embarked upon the first step to being not only a powerful, impactful, influential leader but also a courageous leader.

CHAPTER 7

Transformational Leadership

LEADERSHIP PEARL #7
*Leading today requires the ability to transform . . .
people, situations, and yourself.*

WE ARE IN the middle of a shift in the work environment that is redefining leadership in the twenty-first century. Several forces are converging and driving the shift. Millennials are becoming the dominant population in the workforce; women's voices are being heard in a way they have never been heard before; and employees have an appetite, if not a demand, for transparency in the workplace and are requiring that organizations and professionals have a reflex for change and innovation. In addition, the global social context is being characterized by a consciousness about the environment, governance, people's welfare, and equity, and this is manifesting through consumer demands for the corporate response and voice on these topics.

If you agree with me that there is indeed a shift taking place that is redefining leadership, then you must agree that in order to lead in this rapidly changing environment, one must be a different type of leader, a transformational leader, which requires certain new skills and strategies. If you are sitting in a leadership seat today, you must transform your company's culture, technological platform, supply chain, distribution system, recruiting process, corporate voice, and now, thanks to the shelter-in-place experience that the COVID-19 pandemic demanded, you will have to transform how and where your people work. As we move forward into this new world, you will be responsible for transforming *something*. And if your goal is to become a leader, then you, too, will need to develop your transformational skills, because the pace at which technological and demographic shifts are happening in the world today is only accelerating and I predict that the momentum will continue.

The authoritarian "my way or the highway" type of leader who once dominated corporate America and most other work environments until the beginning of this century just won't work today. This leadership style discourages your team members from contributing their ideas, particularly ideas that could be different from yours. If you are going to develop and exercise a transformation muscle, then you must have access to other people's ideas and experiences. To be successful, you need ideas that are better than yours and you need people who will subscribe to your vision, which will help you execute any transformation. Even the "collaborative and inclusive" leadership style that became more popular since 2000 can't make it in today's world if the leader does not have a penchant or a vision for driving innovation in a decisive way that transforms the organization while inviting and incorporating your team's voice.

Honestly, corporate cultures, in industry after industry, have been in much need of a transformation for the last two decades. As more and more women and people of color obtained outstanding educations and then entered the workforce, a need developed to ensure that corporate cultures offered them equal access to opportunities to learn, excel, manage, and lead, in order for the companies themselves to leverage diversity in a competitive way. Yet, in industry after industry, that has not been the case. Many companies have continued with their old processes and procedures, grossly underleveraging the diverse talent joining their ranks every year. Even companies that thought they were evolving their cultures, by hiring more women and people of color, still did not engage in evaluative studies of their processes and procedures to understand how unconscious biases, for example, might be creating obstacles to equity in the access to opportunities within the organization. Far too many companies and industries continue to have a subjective process for assigning tasks, deals, and projects in the early days of a professional's career, which opens the door for inequities in skills and experiences later. These inequities happen not because there is a true difference in skills and capabilities between majority and minority candidates but rather because there are inequities in the kind of exposure and experiences for professionals, based on race and gender. Companies are just now starting to recognize the cultural transformation that has been sorely needed for at least four decades.

At the same time, innovation has moved from being a nice plus to a corporate imperative, with collaboration and agility now table stakes for survival. This further drives the need for transformational leaders. While innovation has always been a part of any company's growth strategy, the frequency with which new products were created and introduced to the market, or the rate at which model styles and processes change, was much slower than it is today.

As I think back to when mobile phones became mainstream in businesses in the early 1990s, the rate of change was about five years. But it quickly became three or four, then two, and now, a new model is delivered every ten to twelve months. Where long-term consumer contracts were once central to the business model for mobile phone providers, now the business model is driven by completely different parameters. Today, companies are simultaneously working on different versions of products to meet consumer demand for new and better products. Technology has enabled companies to operate with this level of innovation at scale, and quickly. Decades ago, leaders could survive by following a playbook that produced great revenues or profitability. Agility, flexibility, and speed of thought and action were not necessarily required attributes for leadership. The ability to follow the historical playbook was good enough. That is not the case today. Having the skills and attributes of a transformational leader is a requirement to outperform in that seat.

THE TRANSFORMATIONAL LEADER

A transformational leader has four primary traits, which I call the four Ts. A transformational leader is:

1. Thoughtful
2. Transparent
3. Tenacious
4. Transcendent

A transformational leader not only embraces change but also anticipates, instigates, and leads it. A transformational leader subscribes to the notion that change is inevitable, constant, and leads to growth . . . and that growth is good.

The transformational leader is not confined to evolutionary change, which simply builds upon that which already exists, but is comfortable with revolutionary change, which requires a redo, a reset, even a re-create. Revolutionary change requires doing something that is altogether different from what was ever done before. It requires innovation and venturing into unknown product and process terrain. Take the leader of Play-Doh back in the 1930s and 1940s. The company was founded by Joseph McVicker, and the Play-Doh product was used as a cleaner that could remove coal residue, resulting from coal-fired heaters, from wall coverings and other surfaces. As household heating progressed to oil and gas in the 1950s, the demand for the product dropped precipitously and the company almost went out of business. McVicker's sister-in-law, a kindergarten teacher, was using the product for her students in art class and discovered that the kids loved playing with it to make different shapes. The McVickers realized that they might be onto something, a new product they could market to children. They quickly pivoted, changed the color of the product, and one of the most popular children's toys was born. Two billion cans later, the company is still a vibrant asset, now part of Hasbro's portfolio of products.

LEADERSHIP GEM:

Transformational leaders not only embrace change, but they also anticipate, instigate, and lead it. They don't settle for evolving what exists; they revolutionize it.

1. Thoughtful

A transformational leader is thoughtful and strategic. As they consider the need for transformation, a leader conducts a thorough analysis and research about the industry, gaps, changing consumer needs, tastes, and behaviors. As they develop their transformation strategy, they must decide on the what, the how, and the when. At a conference, Pavel Abdur-Rahman, who leads IBM's Data, AI & Technology Transformation consulting practice, explained that in the early 1900s, IBM had been essentially a hardware company that transformed itself into a services company by the late 1900s and to a software company today. This transformation was required as the world was becoming smarter, more connected, and more digital, and the hardware side of technology became super competitive as consumers owned more devices.

The new machines of the early 1900s were expensive and highly valued; fast-forward to the turn of the twenty-first century, and devices were smaller, cheaper, and more mobile. Many new competitors had entered the market for machines, and it was clear that commoditization was next. IBM's leaders at the time, Sam Palmisano and others, saw the trend and made strategic moves to exit businesses that had once allowed the company to lead but could become albatrosses. The company created strategies and processes that would help them to transform.

Transformative and innovative leaders think disruptively. They develop disruptive strategies that attempt to change the way "the game" is played in their industries. In other words, they try to change the competitive parameters in the industry or even create behaviors and consumer appetites that currently don't exist. Take Amazon or Yelp, for example. In 1990, Amazon had not yet been created. The top five companies on the Fortune 50 list were General Motors, Ford, Exxon, IBM, and GE, in that order. In 2021, the top five companies were Walmart, Amazon, Apple, CVS Health, and UnitedHealth Group. In 1994, Amazon came on the retail scene as an online bookseller. Anyone could have surmised that if the company was successful as an online bookseller leveraging e-commerce and emerging supply chain technologies, then at some point it would evolve from selling books to also offering everything from clothes to everyday items.

Very soon after, in 2007, Amazon created a product called Kindle. Kindle was created to bring people more books, digitally. They created the device to house and deliver more books. Prior to Kindle, people read books by purchasing them from a retail bookstore in person or online, or borrowing them from a library. Now you had a device where you could store all your favorite books as well as the books you had yet to read.

If you were taking a plane trip, you no longer had to carry or pack three or four bulky, heavy books. Instead, Kindle allowed you to carry one lightweight device and have all your books available to you. Amazon essentially created a new appetite for *how* people consumed books and other reading material. Over time, other competitors have entered the market, but Kindle has stayed laser focused on the product to drive the appetite for reading, reading, reading. The Kindle is not a replacement for a tablet or an iPad, but they have also created a Kindle app that can be used on those other devices.

I do not think the marketplace anticipated how Amazon the company would strategically move from the traditional retail model of amassing and managing inventory to a third-party seller model. The company now serves the needs of other sellers on its platform, adding another source of revenue to its business model. In addition, it also created a lucrative cloud computing business, which, you could argue, in many ways subsidizes other parts of their business.

While consumers increased their use of the platform to buy other goods, Amazon was also subtly impacting consumer appetites by creating an expectation for one-week, then two-day, then one-day and same-day delivery. Just think about it: It was not that long ago that if you ordered anything by phone or online, you would be ecstatic to receive it on time, typically in about two weeks! Two weeks was the standard expectation and one week was exceptional! Today, if a vendor cannot promise at least two-day delivery, consumers will be looking for alternative sources for the products they need. After all, "Who can wait that long?!" Amazon changed the competitive dynamics of the industry and created a consumer appetite that other companies now must meet just in order to compete.

Like Amazon, another company that drastically changed consumer behavior was Yelp. Yelp was created in 2004, less than twenty years ago, to crowdsource reviews about businesses. At first, it helped users solicit recommendations and reviews from their friends. But quickly, it became a trusted source of information about businesses, restaurants, and the like. Before Yelp came on the scene, the most trusted source of reviews, especially for restaurant recommendations, was Zagat, founded in 1979. Since Yelp was created as an online platform, it encouraged users to write reviews immediately and post pictures as they wrote about their experiences. This created the consumer behavior of people routinely taking pictures of their food and posting about their experiences. The company created an appetite for consumers wanting to share their experiences with the world, including what they ate, where they ate it, and how they enjoyed it . . . or not!

Talk about a change in behavior! Who would have thought that everyday people would want to take pictures of their steaks or cocktails, share with the world where they were eating and drinking, and write a review of the meal. In addition, Yelp simultaneously changed the parameters of competition in the industry. Suddenly, restaurants and other service providers had to be more thoughtful about the consumer's experience as well as work to strategically engage customers to post good reviews or refrain from posting bad ones, as they noticed the power these reviews had to drive their business traffic. This disruptive, transformative company impacted the service offering of many businesses and also restructured the service provider/consumer relationship.

The leaders of Amazon and Yelp were strategic in their thinking as they transformed these companies into the leaders in their respective industries today. At Amazon, Jeff Bezos developed an expertise around inventory management, online shipping, packing, and delivery. He leveraged the expertise that he acquired in collaborations and partnerships with suppliers, and what he extracted from consumer behavior and data, to expand into other businesses and develop other levels of expertise. As he acquired more and more data from customers, the storage and security of that data became important, and Amazon's cloud computing business was born. This business is purported to be even larger than the traditional online business. Talk about transformation.

At Yelp, Russel Simmons and Jeremy Stoppelman figured out that if consumers would take recommendations from their friends, they might also be willing to take advice from people they did not know. If people were willing to review things at the neighborhood level, then they could invite communities all over the world to put forth their perspectives on a whole range of things from restaurants to hotels to almost any service and its provider. They transformed the company from a forum to connect to people you knew to a global community and an online provider of user-generated information that also impacted the vendors themselves.

In addition to how changes might impact consumers and vendors, transformational leaders are also strategic about how changes might affect their team members. As they consider executing a transformation, they must think about whether or not they have the talent needed to do so. As many brick-and-mortar retailers started to pivot to an online presence in the early 2000s, companies had to think about supply chain specialists in a different way.

They had to think about storage and packing in a way that would allow specificity and speed at the same time. They had to think about logistics specialists and the right way to sort and ship customer items to meet customer demand and timing expectations. Where they had previously hired warehouse or logistics professionals, they did not need this kind of expertise. They had to consider questions like: Do you train the labor force that you currently have? Can you do it fast enough to compete, or do you have to go out to find that talent? Do you pay that talent as much as you have paid professionals in that role before? Or is there a different compensation paradigm that must be considered because this is a different vertical in the labor market?

Many transformational leaders are struggling with the question of compensation today because there are many technological changes that must happen industry by industry to keep pace. There are specific skills related to AI, machine learning, data management, cybersecurity, robotic warehouse management, and other roles where companies will need software specialists and other technical professionals that are in short supply and therefore command a different compensation construct. These new constructs are, in most cases, very different from the company's traditional construct. Integrating these new compensation and reward structures into a labor force that has a long tenure and that is most likely used to a very different one can be challenging for a transformational leader.

The transformational leader must also consider who wins and who loses from a proposed change, especially the perceived losers. When navigating the team through the change, they must strategically develop opportunities so that those players can gain something, either tangible or intangible, for both can be valuable to those who might be perceived as losing in the change. It is the intentionality of creating a "win" for those players that will attract those team members to the leader, getting them on board, and ensuring they productively and constructively follow and support any changes. As a leader, it is important that you think through the need for a transformation as well as the process for change. You cannot assume that because you have identified the need to transform a product, service, or other aspect of your business, the rest of your organization will know *how* to change.

In my conversations with many senior leaders over the last three years, it became clear that many knew they needed cultural transformation within their organizations. But the reason they had not initiated it was that they really did not know how. In the financial services industry, for example, in the 1990s, it was clear that firms needed to make changes to the environments on their trading floors to be more accommodating to women and multicultural professionals. However, leaders were afraid that changing the culture would cause them to lose top traders or key salespeople.

At industrial companies, leaders were afraid of disrupting union relationships or losing key senior white male leaders if they sought to make room for professionals who traditionally did not have real access to those roles. Because these leaders didn't know how to make these kinds of changes in a way that would propel the organization forward, they pretty much opted to let the organizations continue as they historically had. They were afraid of "upsetting the apple cart" with transformational cultural change.

A few years back, I had a conversation with a long-only equity asset manager who knew he needed to change his organization's decision-making structure. Several leading portfolio managers worked for the organization. The culture had evolved in such a way that the portfolio managers had the power to do essentially whatever they wanted with their teams, which is generally not the case for a captive asset manager where there are many different portfolio managers with strategies under the same brand roof. These managers not only determined each team member's compensation, no matter what their role or level of seniority and irrespective of the firm's guidelines, they also decided how often they went to see clients, which was different from the firm's guidance of once per quarter. They even went so far as to decide how they would structure presentation books and would often eliminate the firm's branding and emphasize the team's name or strategy instead, which resulted in the teams presenting to clients in a way that was not consistent with the overall firm's brand. The portfolio managers also demanded certain resources from the organization, such as extra office space, the latest version of laptops, expanded expense budgets, plus industry-leading compensation. When compensation time rolled around, they demanded a larger bonus pool for their teams and expanded vacation time. In essence these portfolio managers were extremely difficult to manage and relentless in their demands.

This had become a major problem for the organization because large institutions were increasingly finding value in consolidating assets and were risk averse to doing business with independent money managers, and could not offer additional resources and support in a tough market environment. The large name houses, with highly valued brand names, were winning greater than their fair share of asset allocations. Portfolio managers acting independently were eroding the power of the larger brand and causing confusion among customers seeking to do business with different portfolio managers at the asset management firm.

The leader knew that he needed to make drastic changes to the way things were transpiring. To be competitive in the new asset management environment, he needed to restore consistency to the brand messaging, centralize decision-making, and cut costs. But he was afraid that if he tried to do so, the portfolio managers would leave, taking all the assets in their respective strategies with them and depleting the firm's total assets, thus compromising their leading position in the market. It's important to note that during the year we had this conversation, the market was experiencing negative performance. Most portfolio managers were underperforming, having been caught by surprise by a few geopolitical events that caused the stock market to turn into bear market territory.

There was a bit of chaos on Wall Street; firms were laying off staff. Virtually no firm was hiring. I advised him that it was the perfect environment to call for and implement the changes he wanted to make. No portfolio manager would leave when the market was not doing well. Most asset management clients make allocations to portfolio managers based on performance. None of the portfolio managers were having a great year, and it would be difficult to acquire assets from customers. In addition, in a terrible year, having the resources and capabilities of a large firm is a major asset to a portfolio manager; it can help them ride out the storm, so to speak. Therefore, the likelihood that any of the managers would leave and hang out their own shingles was low. If these portfolio managers were not going to go into business for themselves and would not likely be hired by a competitor in a down market, where would they go? It was the perfect time for him to make the kind of organizational changes he needed to help transform and improve the culture, with little risk of losing his top talent. Chaos breeds opportunity, and this was his opportunity to make transformative change.

Unfortunately, this leader was so afraid of losing talent and impacting the firm's overall assets under management that he failed to make the changes needed to improve the organization and unify and strengthen the firm's brand. The portfolio managers continued to act independently, and the firm's brand slowly eroded. The company lost market share, and eventually he was replaced by a leader who did take advantage of the market environment, successfully implementing the necessary changes in the culture and the governance structure.

Timing, or the *when*, is very important for a transformational strategy. There are some transformations that involve a multiyear strategy, especially if you are trying to do something like what IBM did by transforming from a hardware company to a software and service company. A transformation like this certainly does not happen in one fiscal year. In these cases, it is even more important to have a timeline, so that you and your team stay focused on completion and are not distracted by other short-term priorities.

It is also important that as you plan the transformation, you are as specific as possible about milestones and resource needs. You must think critically about how many tangible things you can do to show and signal pending change and the benefits of that change, especially in the first few quarters of the journey. Presenting a timeline and expectations to your team can solidify the importance and the credibility of the transformation that you are trying to effect. Collectively seeking critical milestones will not only help keep the team focused on progression, but it will also create a sense of cohesion in this common goal of making the company better, more competitive, more profitable, or just a better place to work.

2. Transparent

Whenever you are trying to effect a transformation, transparency is a key and essential ingredient needed to create trust. As we discussed earlier in this book, transformational leaders understand that in order to create the buy-in needed for individual team members or for the entire organization to transform, they need to build trust. First, these leaders define *what* needs to happen. Then, they share *how* the changes will happen and *when* they will be executed. From the start, the leader uses transparency as a way to get feedback and participation in the execution of the change. Even in the face of the unknown, the leader's transparency about what they do and don't know makes team members more comfortable with the change, encouraging them to forge ahead together. A powerful, impactful leader wants everyone either to be an architect of the plan or, at a minimum, to feel they influenced the plan, because when everyone's imprimatur is on the change, the probability of transformational success is heightened.

I learned about the power of transparency to unite and inspire a team from one of the leaders I worked for early in my career. In my role as an operations officer for the department, I worked very closely with this leader. One of his consistent practices was to prepare an agenda for any meeting, whether it was for the internal team or an external client meeting. He also went into every meeting having a point of view about the probable outcome of the discussion, and in some cases, he was very clear about what he *wanted* to transpire. However, he was committed to keeping an open mind in the event that the team's discussion yielded a better idea than his. I once asked him why he was so transparent with all the information. He told me that no matter what was decided in the discussion, he wanted to get the entire team to own the strategy. If for some reason events did not unfold as he expected and the outcome that the team hoped for did not transpire, he wanted everyone to own it, not assign blame to this one or that one, but rather, to win or lose together.

At the beginning of the meeting, he would lay out the client objectives as he knew them, sharing his thoughts and ideas about the different ways the firm could solve the client's problem. Then, he would invite each member of the team to give their thoughts. One by one, he would debate their assumptions, insert other information that only he would know, like the firm's current appetite for risk. He would invite others into the discussion and solicit their ideas as well. In most cases, the team would end up with the solution close to his original perspective, but they would feel that the answer was derived from the discussion and collaborative process.

By being transparent with the information he knew about the client, its tolerance for risk, the size of its capital commitment requirement, etc., he made the team see that he trusted them to do the right thing with the information and keep it among themselves. This further motivated them to work together to arrive at the best solution for the client.

LEADERSHIP GEM:

Transparency builds trust.

This is a very important point. Everyone highly values trust. As I mentioned earlier, getting your team to trust you is key to your ability to lead in all types of contexts, good or bad economic times, periods of high growth, intense environments, or even during a pandemic. If your team feels that you trust them, they will implicitly start to trust you, particularly if you are transparent. The converse is also true. As I mentioned in an earlier chapter, if your team feels that you don't trust them, then they start to feel that there is perhaps a reason to not trust YOU. This will, at best, slow down your momentum toward change and, at worst, impede the transformation altogether. Prior to his tenure, the group had a reputation of being a hard place to work, with very authoritarian leadership. This leader was not only thoughtful and strategic in his approach to managing the group, but he used transparency as a powerful tool to build team cohesiveness and create a cultural change. The department went on to have years of successive record revenue under his leadership.

3. Tenacious

Transformation does not happen without a leader, because environments, especially work environments, don't change by themselves. In the world of work that we operate in, change is happening exponentially faster than ever before. The only way an organization can stay relevant, compete, and continue to win is with a transformational leader at the helm who is tenacious enough to begin, stay with, pivot if necessary, and complete the course of transformation.

Whenever you are trying to transform a culture, process, or even yourself, you must prepare for the long haul. The old saying "Sustainable change does not happen overnight" is true. As you embark on the transformational journey as a leader, there will inevitably be setbacks, obstacles, and naysayers. It is important that you mentally prepare for these things, and you also must make sure that you are physically prepared for the long haul. I am friends with a very successful Fortune 500 CEO who is as tenacious about his physical health as he is about his company's strategy. He once told me that if he is not physically prepared to deal with unexpected challenges—for example, the stamina to withstand the long hours and unexpected, sometimes long global travel that often accompany a crisis and are inherent to a transformation—he would not be able to lead successfully. As the CEO of a company in a fast-paced, dynamic, competitively intense industry, he is often tasked with managing regulatory, legal, and industry challenges simultaneously, while creating strategy and choosing executives who will help him successfully implement his vision. To do so requires him to maintain his mental and physical strength.

Tenacity means that you keep coming back to the plan and working and reworking it until you get to your desired outcome. You must be ready for one, two, or even five setbacks or delays before you reach your transformational goal. Tenacity also means anticipating that there will be times when you will stay in a holding pattern, not moving forward and not moving backward, having reached some level of success but remaining there instead of continuing to progress.

In a company setting, transformation may enter this kind of holding pattern for many reasons. For example, there may be a supply shortage, someone may unexpectedly leave the organization, or, after one year of being on the transformational journey, the board could decide to move in a different direction. Other stakeholders may simply lose patience with this kind of "pause" and want to abandon ship, because they feel the desired outcome was not achieved in the first two or three tries. Sometimes the strategy you deployed does not work as intended and you find yourself needing to retreat and start over again. If you are trying to effect an acquisition of another company, the leader and/or the board may decline your offer several times as they seek higher offers or try to go it alone to create greater value for their shareholders. Either way, your job as a leader is to see the effort through to complete the transformation.

Over the last two decades, there have been many companies that have transformed their business models, supply chains, and internal cultures. Cultural transformations are among the most common kinds we see in the marketplace today, and tenacity is one of the most important tools. The timelines to achieve cultural transformations often span leadership tenures. Technological transformation is probably the second-most-common in today's ecosystem and it, too, often spans leaders. As we discussed earlier in this chapter, IBM is among the best examples of technological transformation. But one could also argue that GM has transformed itself from a car manufacturer to a technology company, and Walmart has transformed from a traditional brick-and-mortar retailer to a technology-driven company. Xerox has transformed from a copy machine company to a document services company, while the Big 4 accounting firms have transformed from traditional accounting to consulting and advisory practices, while maintaining their traditional business lines.

Look at the operational transformation that happened in the music industry. While recording is still a central aspect, the distribution model has completely shifted with a transfer of power from large recording studios to the artist. Technology has enabled artists to stream their content online. Early disrupters like Napster, Sound-Cloud, and others evolved into powerhouses like Spotify and YouTube. Network television companies that once owned all the quality, made-for-television content have had to transform their businesses to create streaming products to compete with Netflix, Hulu, and others. Content creators and large movie studios like MGM, 20th Century Fox, and others have had to transform their models from large budget items to compete with Amazon and Netflix.

None of these transformations happened quickly. The leaders were dogged and committed to making these changes. They developed multi-year plans with detailed and targeted investments in order to achieve the evolution. In almost all these cases, the current leadership had to commit to hiring new talent and even designing new compensation structures to attract the talent. These transformations required skills and capabilities that were outside the company's traditional business models and different from the profile of the company's current success-ful executives. Talk to any leader who has led a successful technological or cultural transformation, and they will tell you that it was a multi-year process that required extraordinary commitment and tenacity. Transforming a company's culture or its technological foundation is not for the faint of heart! In many cases, the leader who started the transformation will not be the one who guides the company once the transformation is complete.

During the most recent financial services crisis, in 2008, financial services transformed from being an industry characterized by outsize risk-taking and leveraged balance sheets to one of increased regulatory guidelines and oversight. We saw many banks restructure their balance sheets, sell ancillary businesses, and focus more strictly on capital ratios and Tier 1 capital and stress tests. We also saw a transition of leadership across many firms.

The leadership profile required in this new environment of heightened oversight was different. It demanded that the leader be extremely comfortable building relationships and answering to regulators and rating agencies, and, frankly, spend an inordinate amount of time with these entities. Just as leaders, prior to the crisis, would spend time with clients, during the crisis they had to build relationships with regulators who took up residence in their company headquarters for a couple of years. As many banks' ratings were downgraded, leaders had to be tenacious in focusing on these key relationships, openly providing information to the market about strategy and performance in a way that leaders on Wall Street had not done before.

In demonstrating tenacity, a leader must exhibit a sense of urgency about the transformation. If your team does not feel that the transformation is a strategic imperative with an aggressive and stated timeline, then the transformation will be vulnerable. I cannot stress enough that when establishing the transformation plan, as the leader you must include a clear timeline, complete with milestones and acceleration points. You must also be relentless about recruiting other key leaders to see and support your vision. No leader can achieve a transformation on their own. If you are not tenacious in recruiting other people to support the transformation, then you leave yourself vulnerable to other competitive groups within the organization that in the best case will not support you and in the worst case will try to sabotage your efforts.

4. Transcendent

In the Oxford dictionary, the word *transcendent* means "surpassing the ordinary; exceptional." If you are to become a transformational leader, you must be able to rise above the inevitable criticism and negative commentary that arises during times of change. There will be plenty of naysayers who will talk about why the change will take too long or won't work. Most ordinary leaders are easily distracted with defending their plans, become discouraged, and may even allow themselves to be dissuaded from moving forward. Ordinary leaders will question and second-guess themselves and compromise the efficacy of the change. This kind of insecurity will undermine your confidence and threaten your ability to successfully execute.

LEADERSHIP GEM:

Transformation requires tenacity and focus; you must rise above the naysayers and remain focused on your end goal.

As a transcendent leader, you must rise above all the noise. You must trust that you have done the analysis, studied the data, and listened to your people and the marketplace about the need for a transformation. It is critical that you keep moving forward, staying singularly focused on the success of the change. Even in the midst of setbacks, you must rise above any disappointing moment and continue to focus on and talk about the vision and the success that the organization will enjoy once the transformation is complete. It is important that, as the leader, you get people to constantly envision "what will be" instead of "what is" in each stage of the process. Your vision and your ability to articulate that vision are critical in order for you to achieve success.

How do you stay above the fray? You must surround yourself with a handful of other leaders who are on board and subscribe to your vision. You will need their intellect to help crystallize the strategy as you move forward, as there will be inevitable pivots. You will need their experience as professionals who might have gone through other transformations, and their expertise in specific areas of the company, the transformation, and their "on the ground" knowledge of the talent who might be critical to the transformation's success and who play a critical role for the future. You will also need their networks and relationships with other experts or talent that might help advance and accelerate the transformation. This small group of people can help to refresh your vision with those whom they lead as well, making sure it remains relevant and a focus. This will give you the support you need to stay above any negative forces that threaten your intentions.

CHAPTER 8

Leading in Times of Crisis

LEADERSHIP PEARL #8
*Visibility, transparency, decisiveness, and empathy will help you to
lead effectively through a crisis.*

As I WRITE this book, the world is in the grip of the COVID-19 global pandemic. As of mid-September 2021, the novel coronavirus, or COVID-19, has affected over 225 million people around the world and caused over 4.6 million deaths in 221 countries. In the United States of America, the disease has impacted nearly 41 million people and caused nearly 660,000 deaths.

In times like this, we look to elected officials and appointees, those who hold what we typically consider to be leadership positions. However, if those whom we have put in those positions fail to inform, direct, or lead, what tends to happen over time is that other individuals start to emerge as leaders and we start listening to them as the voices of credibility or authority, as they provide information, directives, and hope. We almost unconsciously start to follow them. One of my favorite sayings is "Are you really leading if other people won't follow?" So then, the corollary must be true, when others are following you, you are leading!

During this and other crises I have witnessed in my lifetime, such as the stock market crash of 1987, the attacks on the World Trade Center and the Pentagon on 9/11 in 2001, and the financial crisis of

2008–10, I've seen unexpected leaders emerge, people who were in leadership seats who REALLY led in an exceptionally great way, and some who did not. In times of crisis, there are five common things that powerful, impactful leaders do:

1. They are visible.
2. They are transparent, candid, and articulate about the facts that they know and don't know.
3. They are decisive and swift to act.
4. They call a thing a thing.
5. They show vulnerability.

If you are on the planet for any length of time, you will likely find yourself in a crisis environment at some point. Whether you are in a formal leadership seat poised to emerge as a leader, leading a large public corporation or a start-up, I would suggest you consider incorporating these five common things into your leadership playbook.

VISIBILITY

Letting people see you is one of the most important things you can do as a leader. How people view you will determine whether or not they will believe what you say or follow your directives, which is especially critical during a crisis.

As soon as a crisis hits, your priority should be to physically get in front of your people as soon as possible. If it isn't possible to do so in person, use whatever widely acceptable mode of communication is available. While in the past that mode was television or video conference, these days that tool can be social media, such as Facebook, Twitter, or Instagram, or Zoom, Google Hangouts, Microsoft Teams, FaceTime, or some other mobile or digital means of reaching your people all at once.

Think of the major crises that have happened in this country. Each time, the president of the United States of America would appear on television within hours of the event to address the nation. In 2001, when the World Trade Center towers and the Pentagon were hit by terrorists' planes; in 2008, when it became clear that the world was falling into a financial crisis and banks like Lehman Brothers, Bear Stearns, and Washington Mutual were declared insolvent; and even in 2020, when COVID-19 started causing deaths of citizens in China, Italy, Korea, and ultimately the United States, leaders addressed the country.

In 2001, I clearly remember standing on the trading floor with my colleagues as we watched the television screens in disbelief as a second jet flew into the South Tower of the World Trade Center. The managing director who was leading the equity division at the time, and to whom my boss reported, was on the trading floor within twenty minutes, telling everyone to leave the building. While he did not know exactly what would transpire throughout the rest of the day, he knew that terrorists had struck an iconic New York City landmark and that an attack on Times Square (where we were located) was not inconceivable. He knew that the most important thing to do was to get people out of the building and as close to their homes and families as possible. The fact that he came down to the trading floor and was visibly serious about his directive signaled to us to move quickly to leave the building. He didn't get on a loudspeaker; he physically came to the floor so he could look each one of us in the eye. I had no idea where I was going, but I knew for sure that I had to move because my leader was standing before me and telling me to.

In a crisis, by definition, things are unstable. No one knows what is going to happen. The future is uncertain, the outcome of the crisis unknown, and people feel that their safety and welfare are threatened. In general, I have figured out that it is not that people hate change; they fear uncertainty. When uncertainty descends, fear quickly follows as a ready companion, and it also creates or exacerbates the feeling of instability, which in a corporate context can absolutely impede progress and impact productivity. During times of change or crisis, the people in your organization need to see you because you create a perception of stability. In the pandemic, many companies have had to pivot to a different way of working, with many employees working remotely from home and other places. The same holds true in remote environments. You could argue that addressing your people through a screen is a poor substitute for physically being in the same place, which may be true, but it at least provides an opportunity to establish a connection and encourage them to follow you through the crisis.

Hours after the planes hit the World Trade Center, President George W. Bush appeared on television to inform the American people of exactly what had transpired and defined the tragedy as a terrorist attack. A few days later, he flew to New York City and Pennsylvania, both sites where so many had been killed. His address was telecast from ground zero in lower Manhattan. That was important because the country, and frankly the world, was feeling a high level of fear and uncertainty. His physical appearance at the site created a perception of stability. Because he was there, it suggested that nothing else would transpire at that site in New York City. Of course, the president of the United States would not be in a place where a threat still existed. In addition, he outlined his thoughts and intentions about retaliating against the terrorists and declared a war on this terror. Obviously, no one knew what would really happen in the following days, but his visibility to the American people and to our allies around the world sent a message of stability amidst this very real crisis.

When the pandemic overtook the United States, the leaders of New York State and New York City used television, radio, and digital mediums to communicate with their constituents. They even went as far as making daily broadcasts at the same time each day. Why? To establish a feeling of stability amidst so much chaos and uncertainty.

Every day the numbers of infected people and persons dying from the virus were rising and, on some days, rising exponentially. The numbers were scary and no one knew what to expect day to day. But what New Yorkers knew they could depend on was a daily broadcast from the governor at 11:00 A.M. and from the mayor of New York City every afternoon around 4:00 P.M. Each reported on what they knew to be true, the facts, at that time. Many people, including me, came to rely on those broadcasts to understand where things stood with respect to infections and deaths, what the current protocol was, and what the outlook appeared to be at the time. During this period, the country was receiving televised briefings from the federal government, and the information was often inconsistent and contradictory. These state and city leaders became the de facto leaders during the crisis, sharing what individual citizens could expect or should do during this time. It wasn't long before the national cable news networks, including CNN, CNBC, and Fox News, were carrying excerpts, if not the entire briefings, from the state of New York. Soon thereafter, the governors and mayors of other states and major cities started engaging with their constituents in the same way.

LEADERSHIP GEM:

During times of crisis, leaders make themselves visible.

As the crisis of the pandemic continued, leaders increasingly would have medical experts participate in the briefings and stand before the cameras to educate the public about how to stay safe and healthy. Later they would talk about the development and emergence of a vaccine as well as its pros, cons, and any risks. When the vaccine became available, current and former leaders were shown taking the vaccine, to encourage others to do so as well. This visibility was essential to influencing those who were quite skeptical about the vaccine in the early days. Each day, major news outlets displayed former and current presidents of the

United States, the vice president, entertainers, sports icons, and front-line workers receiving the vaccine. As I write this, the visibility strategy is still being deployed as there are still millions of people who have not taken any form of vaccine and the country has yet to arrive at a level of penetration to create herd immunity.

TRANSPARENCY

The weekend of September 12, 2008, is seared into my memory. In the days prior, it had become very apparent that Lehman Brothers, then the fourth-largest investment bank in the world, would not survive another week. Other financial powerhouses, including Washington Mutual and Bear Stearns, were also going under or being purchased and absorbed by larger, more stable competitors, and there was much speculation about what would happen to the likes of Goldman Sachs, Merrill Lynch, and Morgan Stanley, the company where I work. Events were unfolding so fast that it was difficult to tell which bank would be sold and which would crash next.

On Monday, September 15, John J. Mack, then CEO of Morgan Stanley, assembled all the firm's managing directors for a meeting. He told us that he and other Wall Street leaders had been summoned to work with the head of the New York Federal Reserve, Tim Geithner, as well as Treasury Secretary Hank Paulson and others to offer advice and work together to develop a solution to save the other banks.

While he did not yet have a solution for his own company, which with the financial market in a free fall was clearly under the threat of demise, he still called his senior leaders together. He told us about the crisis happening around us, about the activities and discussions he and others at the firm were having with the White House and others. While he could not report on what would happen, because he did not know, the fact that he was transparent and made himself visible gave many of us who were managing other people the resolve to speak to our own direct reports. Because he was calm and confident, we were able to present that same calm and confidence to our teams. No matter what happened, we trusted that he would see us through the crisis or at least "call it as he saw it" and tell us the truth.

Transparency is a sign of strength. It empowers the leader and the people around them. When leaders are not transparent, those who follow them start to wonder if there are things to be concerned about. They wonder what they don't know about or what hasn't been said. They wonder if there is a reason to mistrust the leader who is doing the talking. In the absence of information, people become vulnerable to fear and are easily distracted from the facts. NOTHING spreads faster than fear, and when it starts to spread in a corporate environment, it leads to a breakdown of productivity, trust, and eventually the culture itself, especially amidst a crisis.

One of the reasons it is so important for a leader to be transparent during a crisis is because it is your job to lead people to the other side of the crisis through *and* into unknown territory. By its very nature, a crisis means that there are unpredictable outcomes on the other side of the event, which are usually predicated on several things happening successfully. In addition, it is usually hard to determine exactly how long a crisis will last and whether or not something else will happen that might cause additional complications or impede progress toward ending it.

For example, during the COVID-19 crisis, many stores and restaurants were closed. Schools were shut down. People were asked to shelter in place except to go out for essentials like food, water, and gas. No one knew how long this shelter-in-place protocol would last. Our ability to move beyond it would depend upon the development and introduction of a viable vaccine and then getting a critical number of people to take the vaccine in the hopes of achieving herd immunity or at a minimum to keep people from becoming gravely ill or dying. It was also dependent upon the successful production and distribution of the vaccine, among many other things. The ability to get people to take the vaccine was dependent upon educating the public about its safety and then developing a successful marketing message that would convince them to take it.

One of the keys to getting people to take the vaccine was transparency from the pharmaceutical companies about the research and data produced from the trials. If the pharmaceutical companies had not been transparent about the development of the vaccines, the timeline of when things would be ready, the FDA approval process, etc., it is highly unlikely that they would have been able to get as many people to take the vaccine as we have had to date. Even with the transparency that has been provided to the public, we still have a long way to go.

There are countless other examples of when transparency has been critical to getting through a crisis and also to getting people to trust brands again. One example is J&J's Tylenol crisis in 1982. Despite the fact that the company could trace the deaths of several people in the Chicago area from cyanide-laced capsules to drug tampering in a specific place, they immediately recalled every bottle of the product, ceased production and advertising, and offered customers a replacement product. This kind of transparency enabled them to largely maintain public trust and confidence by displaying a "customer first" mentality, swiftly disclosing information to the public. This kind of transparency enabled them to rebuild the brand and maintain consumer loyalty for Tylenol and other subsequent products.

As a leader in today's environment, you must be comfortable with a degree of transparency that leaders who led organizations twenty years ago did not have to have. If you were a leader in the 1980s and 1990s, part of the value you created was associated with keeping things obscure, marketing the "secret sauce," if you will. Today, however, thanks to social media and the public's appetite for honest, readily available information, you must be willing to be more forthcoming about company strategy, challenges, and even wins than your predecessors. This will not only help you retain your current team; it will also help you attract new talent.

In mid-2020, when it was clear that the United States, in particular, was experiencing a crisis of social unrest, many companies had to articulate where they stood on diversity efforts and their commitment to supporting multicultural professionals, closing the gap in the distribution of capital to entrepreneurs of color, and disclosing data with respect to representation of people of color and pay equity among their professionals.

While many companies were uncomfortable with disclosing such information and, in fact, had never had to do so before, it was clear that silence on these topics could be misconstrued and very damaging to the companies' brand, reputation, or market value. Transparency around diversity issues was key for company leaders and their ability to engage with their employee base and to field customer queries about these topics.

Transparency is a key ingredient to build trust—trust with employees, trust with customers, and trust with shareholders. In a crisis, it is even more important that as a leader you are prepared to be transparent if you want any of these constituents to stay with and support you during, through, and to the other side of the crisis. This holds true whether you are a leader in a large organization or an early-stage company. In a large organization, if today's employees feel that they cannot trust you to deliver on the employer value proposition of fair wages, development opportunities, mobility throughout their career, and fair and equitable access to opportunities, they are not going to stay with your company.

To maintain your company's market share, and certainly to acquire market share, you must be transparent with consumers about the customer value proposition, both when you can deliver and when you cannot deliver. If you are a public company leader, you HAVE to be transparent with your shareholders, especially if you deliver a quarterly performance below their expectations. If your shareholders perceive that you are withholding information or that as a leader you are not being transparent about the problem, your understanding of it, or its depth, they will react strongly and you will experience a swift decline in the company's stock price.

If you are the leader of an early-stage company and you are not transparent with your employees, it could cause you to lose valuable team members at a time when human capital is extremely important to your ability to scale and run the company. It will also likely impair your ability to attract other talent as the early-stage company ecosystem is quite small when it comes to senior talent. If you develop a reputation as a leader who is not transparent, candidates will quickly spread the negative word about you as a leader.

As an early-stage company leader, you are generally only one crisis away from potentially losing the company or having the company face the question of whether it will be an ongoing concern. With respect to your customers, it is even more important that you are transparent when you cannot yet deliver a product or honor the customer value proposition because you are in the process of building customer loyalty. In those early days of your company's life, customers do not offer you the luxury of third and fourth chances to win and retain their loyalty. A customer is more likely to give you a third, fourth, or fifth chance if you engaged with them before you disappointed them, preparing them for what will or might transpire instead of trying to repair the damage after it's done.

Trust is key to retaining customers, employees, and shareholders. Once trust is breached or impaired, it is hard to repair and regain.

I've noticed that some leaders are afraid to be transparent. They fear being wrong or having to retreat from or change something they have said out loud. Do not fall into this trap of withholding information because you are afraid the outcome of a crisis could be different from what you forecast. Your strategy should be to communicate by laying out potential outcomes and probabilities if you have them. Give your audience, your team, customers, or shareholders a sense that you have a handle on the situation by preparing and offering various outcomes and responses to each.

It is certainly possible that something might arise that you didn't anticipate, but when you give an update, you can explain it at that time. In your effort to be transparent, you do not have to cover every potential outcome. The key is to be transparent about how you are viewing the crisis, to articulate what you know to the extent that you can disclose it, and to give your audience a sense of a joint experience or responsibility, i.e., "We are in this together," "I need you with me," or "You know what I know."

During the early days of the financial services crisis, Morgan Stanley CEO John Mack would regularly bring the company's managing directors together for an update on his latest meetings in Washington or calls with other financial leaders. He would give us information that we could share with our teams. In fact, he would give us instructions to speak to our teams about the topics that we discussed as senior leaders. Now, over ten years later, and having read a few books about that time, it is clear that some of what he told us in those meetings was an actual recount of what actually happened in his meetings with other Wall Street leaders. The remaining information was filled with speculation, probabilities, and potential outcomes, some of which happened and some of which didn't.

However, the act of bringing us all together, at least for me, dispelled fear and gave me the ability to speak with confidence to my team and others in the organization. Since he was transparent, I felt I could trust that I would not be surprised and that he and his team were working as hard as possible on the best possible solution for the firm, for all of us. Not once did I panic during those early days, not even when the company's stock price was in the single digits, or the market dropped 1,000 points in one day! Many other leaders in the organization stayed the course in their respective businesses, while a small few worked tirelessly and diligently to arrive at a great outcome for the firm. As a result, the firm emerged from the crisis as one of the strongest on Wall Street. Sure, it had issues to resolve, like many other firms, but on a relative basis, having found an extraordinary partner, we restructured our balance sheet along with a few businesses and emerged as one of the healthiest in the industry.

DECISIVENESS

Generally, in a crisis, the one thing you do not have is time. When a crisis hits, it typically hits hard and fast, and a solution is required quickly. Great leaders understand that while it would be ideal to have all the facts at hand before responding to a crisis, that is usually not the case. Leaders typically must get comfortable and confident making decisions with incomplete and imprecise information and without having clear visibility on the myriad potential outcomes.

Great leaders first avail themselves of all the relevant information as well as leverage every expert appropriate to the crisis that they can find. They quickly assess who is likely to be affected by the crisis, and then, with the limited information they have, they make a call on what needs to be done, sharing a narrative about who will be impacted and how.

As the coronavirus pandemic began to impact the United States, as we had witnessed in China, Korea, and Italy, it was relatively clear that one way to stop the spread of the virus was to quarantine people, limiting person-to-person interaction. However, there was no federal mandate to do so. Despite the fact that there were a few dozen diagnosed cases in the United States, most businesses were still functioning as usual. Airlines were still flying, people were still riding subways and buses, and schools were still in session in most places around the country.

Then, in one weekend, the number of cases tripled and then qua-drupled in New York City. Now the threat was clear and imminent. It was THEN that measures were put in place to limit, but not to stop, person-to-person interaction. Despite the calls for social distancing, we saw images of teens and twentysomethings by the hundreds partying on Florida beaches, we saw hundreds of people walking and biking in parks, and children running, laughing, and playing on playgrounds. That is until the death toll in places like New York City, California, New Jersey, and Florida started making daily headlines. While the de-cision was ultimately made to put tougher restrictions in place, one could argue that if clear directives had come sooner at the federal level, states might have made decisions about putting stay-at-home orders in place much faster, thus stopping the spread of the virus at an ear-lier stage.

After the third consecutive week of new COVID-19 cases in the tristate area of New York, New Jersey, and Connecticut, there were still no federally mandated or coordinated policies and procedures to stem the spread of the virus. By week four of the crisis, the governors of the three states had met to coordinate a response. They understood the power of collaboration and sought to eliminate any arbitrage that would result from people moving from one state to another to avoid restrictions. More important, they wanted to show other states how to design a response that could be mimicked in other areas of the country.

They leveraged the national media to get the word out about their strategy. None of the three knew for sure if their response would be 100 percent effective, but they knew that in the absence of a national directive, it could be helpful . . . certainly more helpful than NO re-sponse or strategy. They did not wait for permission to meet and plan. They assessed the situation with the limited information they had and acted. In the face of the unknown, as a leader, you must leverage your position and show others the way.

Five weeks into naming the crisis as a pandemic, some of the country's most prestigious universities decided unilaterally to not allow students to come back to campus after their respective spring breaks. They knew they could not control where students had traveled while on break, what they would be exposed to, and what they might bring back to campus classrooms and dorms upon their return. This was a particularly bold move, given the many considerations—tuition that students had already paid, education loans already exercised, dorm and dining fees already absorbed, activation of distance learning and the necessary technological capabilities or lack thereof, as well as the postponed or canceled commencement ceremonies.

All considerations aside, they realized that as some of the largest and highest-ranking educational institutions in the country, if they didn't show leadership in this crisis, who would? Who was in the best position to have others follow? Would the leadership of smaller institutions without trustee boards have the courage to make such a bold decision? Great leaders understand that sometimes you have to lead by example to give others the room, the air cover, to make their own decision to act.

Being decisive is key, not only when you are in a crisis but also to divert a crisis. Think about CBS's decision to fire Don Imus in 2007, following comments that he made about the Rutgers women's basketball team that were deemed racist and sexist. There was an immediate adverse reaction from the public, and within days, MSNBC had canceled its simulcast of the show, advertisers pulled out, and CBS announced that it would permanently cancel the morning radio show. If CBS had not acted swiftly following the comment, it could have risked the support of its network and lost millions of dollars of ad revenue for other shows. In the environment we are in, where social media can make comments, pictures, and narratives public and viral within seconds, being decisive as a leader is more important than ever. CBS leaders also acted swiftly and decisively when one of its chief media stars,

Charlie Rose, was accused of inappropriate actions toward women on his team.

He was one of the key anchors on a major morning show and a staple on public TV, making removing him from his role a tough and commercially impactful decision. Rose was a leader in the broadcast and entertainment world, with an audience of tens of millions of women. CBS leaders knew that their leadership in the industry would be threatened if they did not act quickly and swiftly to replace him.

Following the Me Too movement and the murder of George Floyd, we are in a low- to no-tolerance context where leaders are concerned. If there is misconduct or a misstatement about women or people of color that is mishandled by a leader, they will find themselves quickly dismissed by boards of directors. They recognize that an organization cannot prosper or even move forward with inappropriate behavior or comments about women, members of the LGBTQ community, or people of color hanging in the shadows. It damages a company's reputation and can cause a mass exodus of great talent, not to mention expensive legal battles. Decisiveness is a critical tool not only to manage through crisis but also to avoid or mitigate its effects.

We have talked about decisiveness as a tool to avoid or limit the effects of a crisis, but let's also talk about it as a tool for change. Winston Churchill, the prime minister of England during World War II, said in the mid-1940s, "Never let a good crisis go to waste." A crisis is the perfect context in which to lead change. Chaos breeds opportunity, and when things are chaotic during a crisis, people are often distracted, afraid, and confused. It is during these times that you can create the kind of change that perhaps needed to be made before the crisis, but you must be decisive.

LEADERSHIP GEM:

Great leaders look for the opportunity in chaos and crisis.

This is especially true if the decision involves a change that is radical or monumental—you cannot afford to wait.

Walter knew that the back-office process at his firm was onerous, outdated, and very people intensive. Many of the employees had been working for the organization for over twenty years, were very senior, very expensive, and weighing heavily on the company's cost structure. Since the company was the town's largest employer, there would be ramifications if the company scaled down its employee base. But the company was receiving increasing pressure from its shareholders to improve margins. In fact, activist shareholders were circling and calling for the company to restructure its management team and even replace some of its board directors.

In late 2008, it became clear that the country was slipping into a recession and many industries were going to be impacted. It was clear that the company was going to have to lay off workers. Walter had been looking at various technologies that could be used in the company's back office. This technology could tremendously improve throughput cycles, decrease the number of people needed, and, in less than twenty-four months, result in a 200-basis margin improvement! In addition, with the operational improvements and decrease in labor, the technology would pay for itself in less than three years and could drive a longer-term margin improvement. Walter had not implemented this technology before the recession because he and the company's other leaders had struggled with the communication challenges within and outside the company.

As the largest employer in town and one of the largest employers in the state, Walter had to consider what impact this improvement would have on the employees, their families, and the local economy. He knew that many of the employees needed to "upskill" for the new economy, and, frankly, he and the company had ideas about how to do that on a larger scale. In their own interest, they were willing to invest in it to prepare the workforce their company would need in the future.

It had been hard for Walter and the company's directors to figure out a way to even introduce the conversation into the business ecosystem, let alone execute what they knew needed to be done. Then came the recession.

Many companies in the state were forced to lay off workers, restructure their companies, or even close. Walter and his board were decisive about bringing on the new technology, retraining workers even as they laid off workers. They used the shield of the recession and the environment of large layoffs and restructurings to make the changes they needed to emerge on the other side of the recession (the crisis) to improve margins and compete more effectively. When the recession was over, the company was in a position to acquire other competitors, accelerate their growth, hire workers, and advance their plans of building a pipeline of better-skilled labor.

CALLING A THING A THING

I had the honor of speaking to the top six hundred leaders of a Global 250 company a few years back. In the prep call leading up to the event, the organizers said, "We want to give you a sense of what you are walking into before you speak at the event. Our company has been through a really tough time over the last couple of years. We disappointed the Street with our earnings seven quarters in a row, our stock price is the lowest that it has ever been in the last five years, and we have had several restructurings and reductions in force. Most of our professionals have seen their coworkers and friends of many years laid off during the changes. The mood is pretty low and tense. We also want to give you a sense for the run of show. We have a celebrity MC that will kick off the conference, he will be followed by the CEO's presentation, and then we have scheduled your keynote."

I thanked them for giving me the background and asked, "Will the CEO cover some of the things that you just mentioned in his presentation?" "No! No," they quickly responded, "he doesn't want to mention any of those things!"

I immediately thought to myself, what a missed opportunity to lead! How easy it would have been for the CEO to say, "I am excited about this new strategy and believe it will put us back on top to lead this industry. But, before I dive into our presentation, let me address the elephant in the room. We have all been through a tough time. I know that you are hurting, you miss your friends that are no longer here, you are weary with all of the changes, your savings have been hurt by our stock's decline, and you probably are concerned about whether or not we will weather this competitive storm. I know how you feel, because I have had days when I have felt exactly that way. I believe that we can reclaim our position as an industry leader, and I believe that this is the strategy for us to do it. But one thing I know for sure is that I can't do it alone. I need every one of you sitting in this audience today to help me. You are THE BEST that this industry offers, which is why you are sitting in those seats, and if we are going to win this war, I need each of you on the battlefield with me. Are you with me? Are you with me? Are you with me?!"

What was so hard about saying something like this? I thought of this narrative on the fly as we talked on the phone! It was easy to think of and it would've been easy to deliver if I had been in his shoes, because it would have been true. NO LEADER CAN EXECUTE A STRATEGY ALONE!

Great leaders understand that you have to be willing to speak to the good, the bad, and especially the ugly. As we discussed in chapter 6, one of my favorite sayings is "You have to call a thing a thing," especially when the thing is apparent and clearly not good. Your team already knows when something is awry. They know when the company is having a hard time in the competitive marketplace; they hear about it on cable news! They are aware when the competition takes market share or when great talent walks out the door, and they know the reasons why.

As the leader, when you ignore issues and don't address them, you create perceptions that may not be based on facts. In the absence of truth and information, people make up their own stories. When they don't hear from you, your team will speculate that you don't have a clue about what's going on, or that you don't care, or worse, that you are hiding something from them. All this noninformation leads to useless "watercooler chatter" and, ultimately, unproductive behavior or larger retention issues.

As a leader, talking directly to your team members can have a very powerful impact. Whether the topic is competitive challenges, the loss of great people, diversity issues, or changes in competitive dynamics, it says to your people that you acknowledge their fears and hardships and that you are actively trying to do something about them. This is true even if the current solution is just to assemble a team to talk about issues or to access experts to help solve the problem. It gives your people a reason to stick by you and the company through the ordeal.

SHOWING VULNERABILITY

Cecily had to lay off two hundred people, 20 percent of the division. This was the third cut in two years, and if things did not improve, there would be more layoffs in the following fiscal year. She wanted to make the announcement in person and called the employees together for a town hall. As Cecily talked, her voice cracked. She was clearly emotional, empathizing with her employees and acknowledging the hardship this would create for the many employees impacted, as well as their families. She pledged that if there was any improvement in the business environment, she would rehire as many people as possible.

LEADERSHIP GEM:

Leaders who have the courage to show genuine vulnerability and empathy inspire loyalty and support from their teams.

The afternoon following the meeting, her inbox was flooded with emails from employees from across the organization—executives, floor personnel, field salespeople—all saying how much they appreciated her words, her sentiment, and her leadership during this tough time for the company and the economy. Many indicated that not only were they not angry and did not blame her, but they felt that she was doing a great job running the company and steering it through this tough time.

In over thirty years on Wall Street and having endured eight really tough bear markets and recessions, I have repeatedly seen that leaders who own their mistakes publicly, show empathy in tough times, inspire people to have faith, and stick with them as they try to recover get the benefit of the doubt from their employees and the marketplace. Vulnerability is something that we share as humans, whether we want to admit it or not. When you have the courage to show your vulnerability, it is the bridge that helps people connect with you. Allowing yourself to be vulnerable doesn't make you less of a "superhero." In fact, it gives people the opportunity to identify with your humanness, which typically means they respect your superheroism, your leadership, and you even more.

An important part of being vulnerable is to show empathy. Empathy is a valuable tool when you are leading through a crisis. It communicates to your team that you are experiencing the crisis, the tough times, the challenge right along with them. One of the most powerful and effective leaders I know, Ken Chenault, the former chair and CEO of American Express, once said to me during a fireside chat, "A leader's job is to define reality and to give hope." It is a quote I will always remember. Your job as a leader is to be transparent, to be decisive, to therefore define reality, but it is also to offer a view into what could be and to offer hope, and the key that unlocks the door to hope for your team is empathy.

CHAPTER 9

Owning Your Leadership Blind Spots

LEADERSHIP PEARL #9
*Everyone has a blind spot. Identify yours and make it
a priority to eliminate it.*

EVEN THE BEST leaders have blind spots. Blind spots are those situations or areas that are close to you but just outside your ability to see. Leadership blind spots are those areas of development or weaknesses that most leaders are unaware of but that often challenge the leader's ability to fully execute or excel. In some cases, it may lead to a leader's downfall.

There are four common types of leadership blind spots: failure to leverage talent, failure to make personnel changes quickly, failure to prepare the bench-succession planning, and failure to innovate.

1. FAILURE TO LEVERAGE TALENT

One of the most common leadership blind spots is failing to leverage the talent on the team. While many leaders are very good at identifying and hiring talented people, many fail to fully leverage that talent once it's on board. Countless times I've witnessed talented professionals, who have the capacity to perform far beyond the job description of the role they were hired for, idle within or leave organizations, frustrated because the organization or their manager or supervisor rarely asks them to contribute their skills, experience, or ideas.

I know many talented individuals, especially people of color, who have left organizations because they have felt "underleveraged." Too often, they have felt they had more intellect, energy, experience, or relationships that they could bring to their roles, to the organization, or to their boss, but their organization never asked for it, or failed to recognize or acknowledge the other skills and assets they had to offer, even when they were offered. In many cases, these professionals would go the extra mile to voluntarily contribute these assets, but when their contributions were not rewarded or, worse, not even acknowledged, they stopped offering, ending up feeling demotivated or disillusioned.

Gillian worked on Capitol Hill for several years before she joined a leading consumer packaged goods company. She took on a role in one of the company's treasury functions where she excelled in helping the organization lower its cost of financing, developed great relationships with the company's investment bankers, and had a reputation for developing her team. The company found itself in a tough position as pending legislation in Washington threatened to impact one of its most profitable products. If the legislation passed, it would require a change in the sourcing and use of a key ingredient and would negatively impact the product's margin contribution and, as a result, the company's profitability.

Gillian still had great relationships on the Hill and offered to do outreach to key members of the committees and subcommittees that could impact the outcome. Her direct manager told her that this was "way out of her lane" and that she should "let those in government affairs handle the situation." When those executives failed to make any headway in the conversations they had, they enlisted the help of very expensive outside lobbying firms. Even these firms had difficulty accessing key members of Congress, and of those they engaged, they were unsuccessful in persuading them in the company's favor. In the end, the key votes to pass the bill, which was against the company's best interest, came from members who were close relationships of Gillian's from her days on the Hill. Gillian felt strongly that she could have persuaded her former colleagues to more positively consider the company's position and might have been able to change the outcome of the vote.

Greg was a talented lawyer who worked in the bank's litigation department. Since Greg had worked at one of the top law firms in the country for eighteen years before joining the bank, he had a number of corporate relationships. The bankers were very possessive of their client relationships and did not react constructively if anyone even appeared to be infringing on them or suggesting that they had relationships more influential than the bankers.

One day, one of the company's bankers called Greg. The company's client relationship management tool indicated that Greg had a relationship with the CEO of a company that was rumored to be going after one of its competitors. The banker wanted to speak to the CEO and find out if the bank could get hired to represent the company in the acquisition.

Greg acknowledged that he knew the CEO fairly well. The banker asked Greg to make a call to see if he could persuade the CEO to agree to an introductory call. Greg called the CEO and offered a few complimentary remarks about the banker, his team, the firm, and how he thought they could be of service and offer real value to the CEO and his company in a potential transaction. The CEO agreed to an introductory call with the banker, which led to a presentation to the board, and ultimately led to the team and the firm being hired for what turned out to be a very lucrative transaction for the bank.

As the banker gave his postmortem analysis to the CEO, the other senior bankers, and the firm, he focused on the complexity of the transaction, the competitive edge that the bank offered in the competitive process to win the deal, and the overall outcome of the deal. Never once did he acknowledge that it was Greg's relationship that created the opportunity for the firm to even compete for the deal. Greg was never compensated for his role in the deal and never acknowledged for the asset (the relationship) that he contributed to the outcome. As a result, Greg was not interested in contributing his relationships to the firm going forward and decided to stick to what he was being compensated for, his legal acumen and performance as a litigator.

With today's war for talent, losing talented professionals, because they are frustrated about being underleveraged or improperly compensated or acknowledged for the other assets they contribute to the organization, is costly to the organization. It's very expensive in the time and resources necessary to source new talent. Further, it is also a risk to competitive readiness. As organizational needs change, companies spend a lot of time and financial resources to find talent for new needs when, in fact, there are often talented untapped internal resources ready and able to take on more or new responsibility. In most cases, the reassigned talent would welcome the diverse assignment, and in the long run, making moves like these could contribute to increased retention rates.

Let's look at this from a personal perspective. As a leader, when you fail to acknowledge or use all the talent your team members can bring to their role, it costs YOU time, it costs YOU innovative ideas that could enhance your and the team's success, it costs YOU financially as you use your budget to engage outside sources to help you find talent and skills that already exist within your team. Any time you have to onboard new talent, it costs TIME, money, intellectual capital, and resources that could be deployed with a higher return than what new talent can offer, because it takes time to assimilate, train, and integrate new people.

LEADERSHIP GEM:

Great leaders know how to take advantage of their team members' diverse skills and look to reward them.

While I have been discussing failure to leverage talent, let's talk about a derivative idea—failure to reward unique assets that are, in fact, leveraged. In 2020, many companies scrambled and, frankly, struggled to respond to the social unrest that erupted in the country in the wake of the murder of George Floyd and the recognition of long-standing racial inequities in the United States. For the first time, senior leaders within corporations, banks, private equity and venture capital firms, hospitals, universities, and other organizations reached out to their mid-level and most senior professionals of color to help their respective organizations form new employee resource groups (ERGs) to moderate town halls on race, lead conversations among senior executives, and help with other related activities within the company. While many of the leaders of color were happy to be tapped to help with some of these initiatives, many felt a level of disappointment because their unique contributions were not recognized as uniquely valuable at a time when the company needed those assets.

One senior leader put it to me this way. "I have been asked by the CEO to help to form an ERG, lead a half dozen listening sessions, plan a first-ever global inclusion conference, and personally be a resource to speak to younger professionals who are having a hard time with what is transpiring in the streets and the company's response to the current environment, IN ADDITION to my day job. I find it interesting that my colleague who sits right next to me and who does not look like me is not being asked to take on any of this extra work. Yet, in the end, we are competing for the same bonus, trying to achieve the same sales numbers, and working for the same promotion. He does not have all of this added responsibility, but I see no evidence that the company is planning to pay me extra for these new duties. Since they have never had to contend with this kind of external environment, will the organization know how to value my contributions? At what level will they value these contributions? If I am the only one who can execute these 'asks,' shouldn't that be recognized in some way? I don't mind helping, but at this level? How does my report card change from the goals that I agreed upon with the CEO at the beginning of the year?"

At the end of 2020, I reached out to this senior leader to find out if he felt that he had been rewarded in a unique way in exchange for his contributions in this unprecedented, extraordinary environment. He said that while his contributions were verbally acknowledged, his compensation was, as usual, directly correlated only with his sales goals. He did not receive any extraordinary reward or value for his additional efforts to help the firm navigate that year's unprecedented external environment.

As a leader in today's environment, to avoid this gap, you must be innovative and creative in thinking about the value of the attributes a professional brings to the organization that are above and beyond a discrete job description. If you are asking any of your team members to use their other assets (relationships, influence, presence, counsel, etc.) on behalf of the company or the organization, you must fairly ascribe value to those assets. This benefits you by squarely positioning you as a fair, inclusive leader whom great talent will want to work with and for. It also makes it easier for you to find this talent, and, more important, it will inspire people to bring all of who they are into the environment and proactively seek more creative ways to be a value add to your organization.

LEADERSHIP GEM:

When we can bring all of who we really are into an environment, we will always outperform, and that outperformance will benefit you as a leader.

There are three pieces of capital that every professional brings to a role: intellect, experience, and relationships. Great leaders create environments where they can leverage the capital on their teams. But it is impossible to leverage this capital if, as a leader, you do not fully engage with your team, earn their respect, and gain their trust. Any leader who makes this investment in their people will yield a great return on their investment.

How do you avoid this blind spot? First, as you are building your relationship with your team, you should stay current on professional interests of each member of your team. Make sure you understand why they came to the organization, why they were interested in the particular role that they hold today, how they would like to build their career, and what role they would like to ultimately aspire to within the organization. From time to time, as you are assigning different tasks, you should ask about what tasks they found most challenging, what challenges they would like to have, what they would like to improve. I would also recommend that you familiarize yourself with their résumé so that you have a good understanding of their previous experience prior to joining your organization. Oftentimes, professionals are hired into a new role that is different from their previous job or does not leverage their previous experiences. Keep in mind, that professional could also be valuable in a different role in your organization.

Second, when you identify a new need within your department or team, you should first consider the members who are currently on your team, especially those who are performing at a high level. They may have the skills or capacity to learn and perform in the new role. More important, high performers in one role are generally near the point of diminishing marginal utility, meaning they are performing at the highest level possible in that role and cannot do more or do better. A new challenge would give them the opportunity to add new skills to their tool chest or to continue to stay sharp and agile.

Fred had worked for ten years as an HR compensation specialist at a Fortune 500 company. A matrix organization, the company had thousands of roles and specifications, which made defining titles/roles and assigning compensation levels especially complex. Fred had earned a reputation as being particularly good at his job. When he was recruited to another organization, he was hired as an HR policy specialist, and his new duties did not require any of the expertise he had acquired in his previous role. Just after Fred started in the new job, the organization experienced a bit of a crisis and needed someone to develop and define new policies and procedures, and to rewrite the code of conduct for the organization. His new boss focused specifically on Fred's ability to do this particular job, and Fred excelled.

Over the next few years, the organization decided it needed a senior vice president in HR to focus on compensation and engage in a large equity study. The organization wanted to make sure it was compensating men and women equally for executing the same jobs. The company engaged a highly technical executive recruiter to source a list of candidates who were industry specialists to take on this role. When Fred tried to approach his current manager and express interest in taking on the role, he was told they needed someone who had "extensive experience in employee compensation and who understood the technical nuances of complex organizations." Over the last two years, while Fred had established proficiency in his new role, the leader failed to "see" Fred as someone who could handle the complexity of the SVP job. Fred's manager failed to review his previous background and recognize his experience in the space or his reputation in the industry. The reality was that Fred was very quali-fied for the role, but because he was hired in a completely different capacity, the leader failed to really get to know Fred and appreciate his previous background and experience. Fred was not given fair con-sideration. The company eventually hired someone from the outside who did not do a great job. They even then hired a second candi-date whose performance was deemed "okay," but who did not have the reputation in the space that Fred once had. Fred eventually left the organization.

LEADERSHIP GEM:

Before going externally to look for expertise, be sure to see if it already exists on your team.

2. FAILURE TO MAKE PERSONNEL CHANGES QUICKLY

Another mistake I often see leaders make is to not change personnel in a timely manner. Leaders often leave people in roles for too long or don't remove people from roles when it is clear they are no longer pro-ducing at a level the role requires or that the company currently needs. Sometimes it's because leaders are emotionally compromised, feeling loyalty to certain people, those who may have been with them since they founded the company or, in a larger corporation, someone they rely upon as a confidant or have worked with for many years. Rather than make the hard choice, they rationalize that with a "serious con-versation" the person will take guidance and change their behavior and start producing at the expected level. The truth is, sometimes even employees who have been loyal for many years might simply be inca-pable of delivering at the level that is now required, may no longer be motivated to produce outsize results, or have not evolved to meet the company's changing needs.

Loyalty is important, but it cannot supersede what is best for the team and the business. Great leaders must sometimes make hard choices.

In reviewing my own leadership journey, I identified that I, too, have had this blind spot as a leader. There have been times in my career as a manager when I have been slow to replace people on projects, even after it was apparent that I should do so. Frankly, I was surprised about my hesitation, because I am normally very decisive about other business matters. As I reflected on this leadership blind spot and what was causing me to behave counter to my normal mode of operation as a businessperson, I concluded that it was my cultural upbringing.

Growing up as a Black girl in the South, I was constantly told by my parents that I did not have as many chances as other people who did not look like me, that in fact I had one shot to "get it right and I would not get another chance." As a result, I was very careful to make sure I delivered with excellence in everything I did academically, in my extracurricular activities, in sports, arts, etc., so that I could "stay in the game" and be competitive with others. Operating with the thought that I had only one chance led me to put a tremendous amount of pressure on myself. Further, it more than likely tempered my appetite and willingness to take on inordinate risk. I also believe I subconsciously felt that this was unfair and that I deserved to have more than one shot at anything, just like everyone else. Consequently, when I found myself in a leadership position with power, and someone on my team made a mistake or was not performing up to par, and I had the power to give them another chance, I was inclined to do so. And I did, over and over again.

The result of leaving someone who is underperforming in a position for too long is that you are limiting the performance opportunities for other people on the team. Other team members may resent that the underperforming person is not pulling their weight or is being given yet another chance to perform. This resentment will undoubtedly begin to impact other team members' performance. Having to work around a person who is not productive or who is disruptive takes extraordinary effort that could otherwise be invested in higher productivity or innovative execution. The bottom line is that everyone can see that this person is not adding to the team's activities or is depleting everyone's energy and impeding progress, which will eventually cost the team its ability to produce, grow, and advance. Just as important, it reflects poorly on you as a leader.

As a leader, this was not an easy lesson for me to learn, and several times I made the mistake of giving people too many chances before I admitted this was a leadership gap I needed to correct. However, once I owned that this was a problem I needed to address, I moved to fix it quickly. I decided to change assignments among people on the team, removing the person who was causing discord and not performing as expected. The result was an immediate improvement in team morale and dynamics and an increase in overall productivity.

As a result of my own experience with this particular leadership blind spot, I recommend a leadership best practice of taking the time to review your relationships with team members with another leader outside your area of expertise. You should do a verbal review of your team members' strengths and weaknesses and have this person interview you about each candidate and challenge each of your assessments, particularly the positive attributes that you ascribe to your direct reports. In this conversation, if the person is asking you the right questions, it will be easy to hear when you are making excuses for people, rationalizing their behavior, and perhaps overinvesting in their career.

LEADERSHIP GEM:

As a leader, get into the habit of reviewing your team members'
performance with a leader outside your area of expertise to be sure you
don't have any blind spots about their performance and impact on the team.

Another best practice is to have members of your board's compensation and talent committee undertake this process with you. No matter what process you choose, it is important that you have a mechanism in place to make sure you have not developed a blind spot about professionals whom you have been working with for a while or whom you may be unfairly giving too many chances to correct their performance or behavior, to the detriment of the rest of the team members. We are vulnerable to our own experiential and cultural biases, even as leaders, and as we know, biases become major obstacles to productivity and performance in a work environment.

In chapter 1, I mentioned a wonderful speech I heard from Meg Whitman. Among the many wise things she said was "One of the most important jobs that I have as CEO, if not the most important job that I have, is to make sure that the right person is in the right seat at the right time." She suggested that while Mike and Raj might have been the right people to create the opportunity, and even were the right people to bring the idea to fruition and operational reality, neither of them might be the person to grow and scale the opportunity. It is the leader's job not only to recognize that fact but to do so in a timely manner that will not compromise the momentum of the project's time to market and the company's competitive position.

Tim and Ed founded a technology company that could be the next unicorn in the industry. Tim was the lead salesperson and Ed was the chief product engineer. The company's product was an AI-enabled platform that would enable the tailoring of a product's sales narrative according to end users' needs. There was no other product on the market that had these capabilities, and it had use cases in technology, financial services, and consumer packaged goods. The company had successfully raised several rounds of financing but was at a critical point in its growth. Prospective investors in the next round wanted to see if the company could make sales to large-enterprise customers. From its inception, the company had found tremendous success with small and medium-size enterprises that were largely Tim's relationships from his previous corporate roles. But in order to progress, the team also had to prove to the investor community that they could penetrate larger enterprises, as this was the market segment that offered explosive growth opportunities for the company.

After compiling a large list of target customers and after several months of trying unsuccessfully to get meetings with the key decision makers within the targets or failing to close on the meetings that they were able to secure, Ed knew that Tim was not the person who could take the company to its next stage of development. Since they founded the company together, Ed did not feel that he could tell Tim he needed to consider a different role within the company or, worse, that they should hire someone to replace Tim in his role as the chief revenue officer and in his capacity of driving the company forward. Ed tried holding strategy meetings with Tim, they tried different strategies and even engaged sales consultants, but still Tim could not close on an account. Quarter after quarter passed and not only were they not bringing on new customers, but Tim was also failing in his attempt to get renewals from existing customers. Ed engaged some of the advisors to the company who tried to tactfully suggest to Tim that he may not be the right person to drive the company to the next level. But Tim made excuse after excuse for why he was not able to close the sales.

After several more quarters, the company was in trouble. It could no longer make payroll and did not have money to invest in product upgrades or new product development. The company was sold for a fraction of the value of the last round of financing.

If you are a co-CEO in an early-stage company and you are running the company with one of your founders, it is even more critical that you have an outside board of advisors or, even better, a board made up of dispassionate investors, who, while they care about the company's success, are not so emotionally tied to either one of the founders. They must be able to make objective, unemotional decisions about what is best for the company. It is really hard to divorce yourself as a leader when the product or company is something you have created. One of the ways I overcame this precise leadership blind spot was to focus on the fact that the product I had created at the firm had a real future. In fact, I knew it could become part of the firm's growth strategy to continue to attract bright, young, entrepreneurial-minded professionals to the bank. I changed the definition of success from putting points on the board to maximize my bonus in any given year to having this product grow in perpetuity and become another source of revenue and attractiveness for the firm. In embracing this definition, it was clear then that my best and highest use was to put real leaders in place who could take the effort and the group to where it needed to be ten years from now, when I knew I would no longer work at the company. I did not focus on what I was giving up but rather what I was building to outlast my tenure.

There is another instance when failing to make personnel changes can quickly become detrimental to you as a leader: when you have ascended to the leadership seat and have inherited the entire team from your predecessor. I referenced this point earlier in the book, but let's go into a little more detail here. Living in New York City for several decades, I had the opportunity to witness New York City mayoral races, state elections, and other special elections and study closely what happened when there were leadership changes, especially at the mayoral and gubernatorial level. One of the things I noticed is that as soon as a new mayor comes into office, they will let go of all the existing deputy mayors, who were running large agencies or key city operations, and replace them with new deputy mayors. This was true even if the existing deputy mayor was doing a great job. I also saw this at the federal level, when I was appointed by President Barack Obama to run the National Women's Business Council during his second term. Toward the end of the term, many of the other presidential appointees began vacating their roles because they knew the next president would appoint his or her own people. I stayed on through the election of

Donald Trump so that I could finish a few initiatives we had started. But sure enough, within the first year, the new president named his own head of the council, mainly because I had been appointed by the previous president. Despite the fact that the council had accomplished a number of great things in the preceding few years, I was replaced.

After watching this phenomenon over and over again, and experiencing it myself, it became clear that "when you are the new girl or guy on the block, you must surround yourself with your own people." Doing this gives you the best runway for surviving and hopefully thriving as a new leader. If you are surrounded by the last leader's people, then you can't be sure the team will support all your endeavors, give you all the information you need to lead effectively, or, frankly, give you their very best efforts and contributions. The assumption is that this old team is loyal to the old leader and not to you, and that the people you prospectively choose will be loyal to you and in effect "have your back" as you lead in this new role. If you are constantly looking over your shoulder, it will limit how far you move ahead.

LEADERSHIP GEM:

When taking over the lead of a new team, it is often necessary to "clean house" and bring on your own people who are loyal to you and supportive of your efforts.

Practically, however, in a corporate environment or even in a philanthropic environment, you cannot just walk into a new leadership role and dismiss everyone. In fact, it could be detrimental to your ability to lead because some of the team members you inherit may know more about the product or the process than you do. You may have been brought in to inspire, organize, or build a strategy, not because of your functional expertise, and you will need people on your team who have the "know-how." As a new leader, your strategy should be to quickly assess which of the team members are extremely loyal to the last leader and are not open to learning from or about a new leader. They are not apt to be supportive and fully contribute in the way you need. You should also seek to understand those team members who might have vied for the leadership role and lost out because senior leadership or the board chose you. You want to quickly understand whether that person will be committed to working constructively and productively under your leadership. If there is a chance at all that they are reluctant to do so, then you must move quickly to reposition them in another role at the company or to help them find a role outside the organization. The issue is that this person will present a constant threat to your leadership efforts whether it is real or imagined, and either way, it might distract you from focusing on leading as effectively as you can.

Tyler was the new CEO of one of the highest-profile nonprofit organizations in a major city. The charity was created to focus on providing ancillary health and economic services to communities with large underserved populations. The previous CEO, Charlie, had done a great job establishing a leading brand profile for the organization, increasing the number of people served, putting the organization on a solid financial footing, and building an organization of loyal professionals. In its five-year strategic plan, the board decided that it was time for the organization to focus on affordable housing and community centers that would provide these ancillary services as well as job training, computer and financial literacy, after-school care and education, and tax preparation. The board realized that the organization now needed a leader and staff who understood real estate tax credits and could build strong relationships with state and city leaders who might provide creative real estate options.

When hiring Tyler, the board chair, Richard, told him that even though Charlie was retiring from his role in leading the organization, the board had decided to give Charlie an office for a year in the same building for him to work on his other endeavors, and that it might also allow for a smoother transition.

At first, Tyler was fine with the idea, but within the first sixty days, it was clear that having Charlie in the building was disruptive to Tyler's leadership in the organization. Charlie would ask to sit in on staff meetings, albeit in the back of the room, but still in the room. Staff members would often seek his opinion on something that Tyler had requested from them. Charlie could often be found walking the halls or sitting in someone's office chatting and shooting the breeze. While on the surface everything seemed to be going fine, it was not long before members of the team started going to Charlie for advice and counsel more than they were engaging with Tyler.

In the first sixty days of Tyler's leadership, he had accomplished quite a lot. He leveraged his relationships with key real estate developers, locating attractive property for the nonprofit at an advantageous price. He was also able to leverage his political relationships to garner great concessions from the city and state, and the board was extremely impressed that Tyler could accomplish so much in such a short period of time. They concluded that he would absolutely be able to execute the board's strategic vision.

Tyler knew that to get the team to align and execute his action plan, he would need to get Charlie out of the building sooner than the time frame the board had promised Charlie. Tyler went to the board chair and said, "I believe that in this first quarter, I have been leading the organization in such a way that I have proven that I can execute as articulated in our interviews. However, I believe that I can do an even better job than what we have discussed, particularly if I can get the full focus of the team behind me. While I know that the board has given Charlie a space in our headquarters over the next few months, I believe that it will be more productive if he is not in the same space as the team and I. Since it is the space he needs, I have taken the liberty to find a really attractive office for Charlie to use that is located just three buildings down the street. It will be best for our execution timetable if he moves to this new office." While the board chair was reluctant to move Charlie after working with him for many years, he also did not want to risk compromising Tyler's ability to continue to execute the plan. He asked Charlie to move to the new office space.

If Tyler had not acted when he did, he would have put at risk his ability to build relationships with the team and execute his vision, and he ultimately might have disappointed the board or fallen short of their expectations. If you are a new leader who is taking on a role from another strong leader, you have to move quickly to engage your team, enlist their support of your vision, and solicit their input to further tailor and refine your plans. When everyone's fingerprints are on the blueprint of a new leader's vision, everyone is equally invested in the success or failure of the plan, and the transition goes from YOUR vision to OUR vision and strengthens your opportunity for success.

3. FAILURE TO PREPARE THE BENCH

Many leaders do a poor job of preparing the bench—training and exposing their direct reports to opportunities so that they'll be ready to assume the leader's job once they leave. Since it's obvious no one can stay in a job forever, the question is "Why?" My theory is that there are two reasons. First, some leaders are reticent to actively and assertively do succession planning because of their own insecurity. They worry that the board of directors will think the person in training is a better leader or that the trainee will make a play for the leader's job. Second, some leaders fail to adequately train their successor because the board of directors, shareholders, and advisors have not made doing so one of the leader's priorities as part of their annual performance evaluation.

One of the most important best practices of corporations today is, at least once a year, for the board of directors to ask the CEO to prepare a report or presentation on the top three to five people in the organization who could replace the CEO should it be necessary.

It is prudent for every organization, whether a for-profit or a not-for-profit, to make sure that someone within the organization is ready to ascend to the leader's position, or to do active planning to get several candidates ready. If there are capable candidates, but they are deemed not yet ready, then the CEO must set a timeline and lead the organization by planning assignments and arranging experiences or geographic exposures to get the candidates ready.

As a leader, you should think about at least three candidates who could take your place in the organization and be intentional about investing in their candidacy as a successor to you. In today's environment, where most large companies are operating on a global scale, it is important to make sure that your candidates have global exposure, either running a business or department in another country, managing a multinational team, or soliciting global customers. If a candidate has had only domestic experiences, they are likely to be handicapped in their ability to manage and lead other professionals with different backgrounds and skills. It is also best practice to make sure that the candidates have financial, operational, sales/customer, management, and leadership experience as well. Ideally, you want the candidate to have had exposure to those parts of the business that are major parts of the organization's revenue engine.

The reason I recommend that you invest in at least three candidates to succeed you is that in today's competitive environment, where there is clearly a war for talent, especially female and multicultural talent, you and your company are under the constant threat that another company or organization may poach your best people. The last thing you want to do is overinvest in one candidate to the exclusion of others and then have that candidate surprise you by taking another job offer that you did not see coming.

Sarah and Jim were two of the best leaders in a global technology company. Sarah had responsibility for the domestic business, which accounted for 40 percent of the company's revenues and profitability.

Jim had responsibility for the Asia Pacific business, which accounted for the remaining 60 percent of the company's revenues and profitability. When asked, the CEO, Hal, was always quick to say that Sarah would be his choice for CEO if something were to happen to him. Sarah, however, had no experience running any major business outside of the United States during her eighteen-year tenure with the organization, while Jim had held significant roles in the United States and Asia Pacific. To an objective observer who reviewed both Sarah's and Jim's résumés and summary of experiences, it would appear that Jim was the more obvious choice to succeed Hal because he had over twenty years of experience, had worked both domestically and internationally within the company, and was a respected leader throughout the organization. Hal knew, however, that there were particular skills around sensitive company issues that Jim needed, but Hal never seemed to develop experiences or assignments to provide what Jim needed make him an equivalent candidate to Sarah.

One day, Hal was accused of an illicit, nonconsensual act toward another employee, and in keeping with the board's no-tolerance policy, he was removed from his role as CEO until everything could be resolved. At the same time, Sarah told Hal and the board that she had accepted an offer to work at a rival company and she could not be persuaded to stay. The board gave Jim the role of CEO, but because Hal had failed to provide Jim with the experiences or exposure he needed in specific areas, he was not fully ready to handle the rigors of the global role of CEO of the company. The company stumbled significantly as Jim tried to lead it in executing Hal's plan, and it lost significant market value before Jim had to be replaced with an external CEO candidate.

As a leader, you always want to give yourself a choice of candidates to succeed you because there is always the unknown of the competitive environment for talent. Part of your legacy as a leader is the person you choose to succeed you, should you have the honor and the luxury of helping make that decision. I have often marveled at leaders who have nominated candidates to succeed them who were obviously weaker than the leaders themselves. As I have seen this occur many times, I have wondered whether a leader's motivations were (a) to have the organization miss them when they were no longer there (emotional, ego-driven), or (b) to hurt the organization in some way (emotional), or (c) just poor judgment. No matter what the reason, it was clear that the leader did not understand that their choice for a successor reflected on them and would be part of their legacy at the organization.

When I look at the leaders I admire, part of the reason I admire them is that they have been very intentional about putting someone in their seat who they thought would do an even better job than they themselves did. It speaks to their focus on what was best for the company or the organization, their understanding of what true leadership means, that it is not all about them but instead about the best interests of those they serve. It is about their desire to have a legacy of excellence that surpassed their time in the leadership seat, that would carry forward with the leaders that followed.

If for some reason the board does not believe there are any appropriate internal candidates that could, with training, take on the leader's position, then the board and the current leader must move quickly to recruit one or two people who could be groomed to take on the top spot. It is not about creating a threat to the current leader, or even keeping him or her accountable. Rather, it is the board's duty to the shareholders, or, in the case of a nonprofit, to its funding network and constituents, to make sure that the organization could operate continuously in the face of losing a leader.

4. FAILURE TO INNOVATE

Throughout this book, we've talked about the importance of innovation in every industry. Whether it's healthcare, technology, financial services, retail, or any other, failure to innovate will lead to failure to thrive or exist. I can think of many companies in my lifetime that were industry leaders, once deemed iconic—Polaroid, Blockbuster, Kodak, Sears—that failed to adopt new technology, read the changes in consumer tastes, or create consumer appetite for new products, and have gone or are going out of business.

It is the leader's job to be essentially maniacal about innovating in order to preserve and ensure the organization's future. Yet, many fail to do so because they fear failing and losing their leadership seat, when the reality is that if they fail to innovate, the competition will assume the company's market share, the stock price will fall, and the board will remove them as leaders anyway. Many others think, "Change is too hard; the person before me didn't do it, why should I take this on? Why introduce this element of risk with this board?" Still others fail to innovate because the forecasted benefit of the investment required to make the change will not likely come to fruition until after they have retired or moved on to another role.

In any case, when a leader fails to innovate, they expose the organization to an increase in competitive threats from which the organization may not recover. By the time the increased threat is realized, it is generally too late to marshal the proper technological, financial, and people resources to credibly respond to a competitor's advances. In many cases, the organization has already started to lose good talent to its competitors or to upstarts, and the general morale at the company is starting to sag, making it very difficult for the company to reenergize the workforce to pivot toward change.

An obvious example of this is the retail industry. Amazon came onto the retail scene as an online bookseller in 1994. First of all, no one thought that an online bookseller would disrupt the bookselling business, let alone create a consumer appetite for one- and two-day delivery of all kinds of goods. Look at the clothing, perfume, shoes, hardware, and other specialty verticals within retail that failed to invest in delivery, online shopping, or carrying third-party products. Look at the luxury brands that thought the quality of their products and the value of their brand name could transcend common consumer demands and that the appetite for in-person shopping would remain robust. In 2019, 9,300 stores were expected to close, including names that had been around for decades, such as Sears, Kmart, A.C. Moore, the iconic Barneys in NYC, and this was before the COVID-19 crisis caused thousands more to shutter their efforts as retail foot traffic came to a screeching halt amidst a shelter-in-place protocol for the pandemic. Many of these companies failed to innovate and invest in their supply chain, in online retail and delivery capabilities, so as consumer demand for online shopping and home delivery grew, these companies could no longer compete. As the stores closed, the brands faded and the leaders lost their seats.

On the other hand, consider the financial services industry and how many of those leaders have continued to innovate and thrive. Over thirty years ago, equity and debt securities trading had huge margins, think forty to fifty cents per trade, and many of the trades were completed using manual spreadsheets, making for a very people intensive business in the back office. Sales and trading business were clearly a part of financial services that could be tremendously improved with the integration of more technology. With the rise of spreadsheets and other programmatic trading, the trading and settlement process was even more ripe for technological disintermediation. Over the next two decades, technology completely transformed traditional trading, and the execution of a trade went from forty or fifty cents to pennies and then to fractions of a cent. The entire business went from a specific trade business to a volume game. In addition, as the industry started to consolidate (and every industry does at some point), those firms that had made the technological investments and, as a result, had experienced tremendous market share growth and profitability were in a position to acquire and absorb the businesses that had not made those investments.

In addition, when the financial services crisis happened in 2008, those smaller firms were even more vulnerable and many did not survive.

As I have said throughout this book, innovation is the dominant competitive parameter across all industries. Failing to innovate as a leader in today's environment is detrimental to your organization and to your success as a leader.

LEADERSHIP GEM:

Great leaders are always questioning the status quo and asking, "What can we do differently and what can we do better?"

As a leader, you must be on a constant search to answer the questions: What can we do differently from what we did last year, last month, last week? How can we change our customer experience? What is the customer saying to us about what is important to them? If I were going to disintermediate our company, how would I do it? In our ecosystem, are we the middlemen? How can we change our standing to move out of the middle to the role of originator or closer, for the middleman always gets eliminated? If we are doing really well, having years of record performance, what could happen to change that? Where are we vulnerable? What is the most vulnerable part of our business? Even if we are leading on every competitive parameter in our industry, how can we do it differently? For the last few years, I have been challenging leaders to approach each day with a "blank sheet of paper" mentality, which means, if I were starting this business today, what would I do differently, knowing what I know now about the industry, about the availability of talent, about the changing demographic in this country, about the role of technology in our industry? What partnerships would I foster? How would I collaborate with competitors? With emerging companies? How could I make this a more attractive environment to work in?

I once asked a university president if he had a "blank sheet of paper committee" within the university. He looked at me with a little smile and said, "What is that?" I said, "If you expect the university to maintain its leadership for the next one hundred years, then the best minds from within each discipline, in economics, philosophy, history, English, education, law, business, should be thinking of how we can change higher education. What would you change about the university's course offerings, engagement with students and faculty, on-campus versus online learning, if you were creating the institution today?"

His answer to me was, "We have been around for over one hundred years and we have been successful in engaging our alumni and other institutions and have raised a record amount of money. I would say that we are doing something right, and it is not easy to change higher education."

I was stunned by his answer, which implied that he was not focused on innovation in the way he should have been. The reason I had asked the question is that I had just finished a phone call with an icon in the technology, media, and entertainment industry who was trying to recruit me to an advisory board for a company he was building that would disintermediate higher education as we know it today. If he is successful, in five years, this university could easily find itself vying for the best and the brightest students in a way that it does not have to compete today. Today's college business model is driven by students in seats, bodies multiplied by tuition dollars. What happens when the number of bodies declines? You can do the math!

Given what you know about the importance of innovation today, there is no excuse for you to be vulnerable to this leadership gap. If you cannot find something in your company or organization that you need to change or improve, then you should understand that you might have a blind spot. Identify it before someone else does!

CHAPTER 10

Taking the Journey from Oversight to Insight

LEADERSHIP PEARL #10:
*Strong insight will lead you to focus on
and execute what will be instead of what is.*

WHEN I STARTED my career journey over thirty years ago, leadership and management were almost synonymous. When people spoke about management, they were largely referring to those who held leadership positions. Since then, many books and articles have been written that make clear that there is a difference between the two.

For example, a variety of business literature defines management as an entity that controls or guides processes or a group of people who work to accomplish a goal. On the other hand, leadership involves influencing, motivating, and enabling others to contribute toward a defined endeavor or success.

In addition, about five years ago, the Executive Leadership Council (ELC), a national organization comprised of current and former Black CEOs and senior executives from Fortune 500 and Global 1000 companies, commissioned a paper, *21st Century Global Leadership: Global Black Leaders Speak.* The ELC works to open channels of opportunity to develop Black executives to positively impact businesses and communities. According to the research, the key success factors for leaders in the 1960s, 1970s, and arguably through the 1990s involved oversight. In other words, leaders during this period were expected to envision, enable, and execute a clear, well-thought-out, documented plan and to ensure there were few if any deviations from it. A manager who could formulate a plan, create a budget, assemble a team, and "get the job done" was considered a leader.

However, the ELC survey, which included input from executives in corporations across several industries, revealed that today's sought-after leaders, those considered to be impactful and effective, demonstrated insight. For example, insight about how to potentially solve a problem, insight about what the next iteration of a product or a process might look like, or insight about challenges or obstacles that could arise in certain situations. Nowhere in the paper did anyone define someone to be a great leader who offered step-by-step instructions about how to complete a project or execute a plan. A strong manager, yes, but not a strong leader.

The definition of leader had clearly shifted over time, pivoting from oversight to insight. Part of having and demonstrating insight is knowing when it is time for you to distribute your power. Leadership is a journey from execution to empowerment. Essentially, it is about letting go of the tasks and assignments that you once executed well, the stellar way you performed your work to earn that promotion and a seat of authority, and deliberately and intentionally passing them along to others. As you free up time and energy that allow you to focus on important aspects of the business such as high-level strategy and long-term planning, for example, this offers your team members the opportunity to develop, outperform, earn a promotion, and become leaders themselves.

LEADERSHIP GEM:

Never do anything that someone else could do. Leaders step away from execution so that they can focus on enabling and empowering their team and organization.

Leading is about empowering other people and illuminating the path for them to uncover their own greatness and how they can best make a contribution to the organization and, in the process, acquire enough knowledge to train and prepare others for leadership in turn.

To be a powerful, impactful, and influential leader today, you MUST invest time in developing those who you know have the skills to execute the tasks at hand, but who, more importantly, you believe have leadership capabilities. This also requires insight . . . insight about other people. As a leader, you must be able to see beyond what skills they have today toward what they might be able to offer after further investment in their training, leadership development, and increased exposure. This level of insight will require that you invest in yourself and your EQ, or emotional quotient. Leadership requires ongoing personal development, too. Continually learning more about yourself and how you relate to and evaluate other people is a key component of insightful leadership. Many people are excellent at execution. However, they often have a hard time making the jump to being an outstanding leader. Insight requires evaluating people beyond their responses to perfunctory interview questions as well as the ability to effectively train and develop people.

To be fair, many who are sitting in leadership seats today, members of the Baby Boom and Generation X demographics, likely advanced in their careers reporting to "my way or the highway" leaders. They were taught to execute, execute, execute, and were not trained to listen, have empathy, read other people, or be authentic in their interactions. Therefore, they became leaders without developing this important component of the insight muscle. This level of insight is required of leaders today and many are struggling, in this environment of global pandemics and social unrest, with how to lead a younger workforce that demands these insight leadership skills.

This kind of insightful leadership is becoming table stakes, particularly in industries where people are the primary assets. Part of your job as an insightful leader is not only to anticipate potential developments in your business but also to get to know and understand your people and how they might react and respond in potential scenarios and situations. In your position, you can act as a safety net to those you are developing, by teaching and allowing them to take risks, fail, and recover. Your role is to help them to further develop their judgment and decision-making skills.

Here is where your job of providing insight makes a sharp departure from oversight. As a leader focused on oversight, your primary role is simply to make sure that people are doing and executing as they have been directed. However, as an insightful leader, you are looking beyond execution, providing guidance and direction, yes, but also evaluating whether your people are defining the right issues, problem-solving in a creative way, innovating, and anticipating the next course of action. Are your people setting up situations to create momentum and forward motion on their project, or are they completing a list of predetermined tasks?

Your job is to help them form the habit of thinking ahead, getting comfortable taking risks, even pushing them beyond their current skills and letting them fail, and then watching how and if they can recover, helping them refine their resilience muscles. Further, you must coach them on how to coach others.

Simone was an outstanding executor. She received an outstanding performance rating on all her evaluations throughout her career, from her first entry-level associate position through her latest promotion to executive vice president (EVP). As a newly minted EVP, her job was to run the business development team, a new group within the company. Her team's job was to scour books, short films, and other media that could potentially be purchased by her company and later developed into entertainment content for television, the big screen, and streaming platforms.

Simone was also responsible for hiring her new team. While she had previous experience interviewing candidates as a part of her company's campus recruiting program, she had no background recruiting and hiring a team of her own and had never been evaluated by the company as a leader. In the past, when she interviewed candidates, she evaluated their backgrounds and ability to fulfill aspects of the specific job description, and she assessed their level of initiative and ability to be a self-starter. When she started recruiting for her own team, Simone followed the same playbook.

Simone hired four talented people for her new business development team, two at the vice president level and two in more junior roles as senior associates. Her intention was that the VPs would help to train and develop the more junior associates and that she would leverage the VPs' skills for herself. For the first six months, things went smoothly. The team had a list of specific goals and accomplished them easily. However, as time progressed, the department's role in the company evolved. Simone and her team were asked to take on additional responsibilities. Much of what they were being asked to do was new for Simone as well as for the rest of the team, and the workflow was intense and high-profile.

As she worked to integrate herself more with other senior leaders and learn to anticipate her boss's expectations, as well as the expectations of her boss's boss, Simone delegated much of the work to her team. She automatically expected that they would know how to execute. The team quickly became frustrated. The VPs did not know how to perform many of the assignments she gave them and when they looked to Simone for help, she acted as if she was exasperated at their inability to perform. The poor senior associates were equally confounded because they could only execute when the VPs assigned them projects. Work quickly backed up and deadlines were missed. The culture of the team soon became toxic, and because of the team's high visibility, Simone's inability to lead became evident to the organization's more senior leaders.

How could this happen to someone who had spent their entire career in the organization and was previously considered a superstar who demonstrated nothing but outstanding performance? Upon closer examination, it is obvious that Simone had never had the opportunity to be trained and developed as a leader and trainer of other people. She had been rewarded throughout her career for her ability to deliver upon discrete and high-profile assignments, but she was never evaluated on her ability to choose, grow, retain, motivate, and inspire a team. When she became an EVP, she was virtually untested as a leader and now she was promoted into a seat where building a team and leading people were an essential part of her job and what she was expected to deliver for the company.

If Simone had insight into what the new job would require, including her current skills and ability as an executive and emerging leader, she might have thought differently about her people needs. If she had taken the time to assess and identify her own gaps or even had access to tools that might have helped reveal them, she would have recognized her needs as a leader. Simone used the same criteria in choosing her leadership team as she did when recruiting on college campuses. That was a mistake.

She had chosen great "soldiers" or executors, people who, like herself as an individual contributor, could get the job done. But what she needed was people who were creative, self-motivated, and able to execute without much direction. Her team needed strategic thinkers who could develop and apply solutions to work they had never done before.

If you ever take on a newly created role, as Simone did, it's important to recognize that no one really knows what the ultimate report card will look like. You must be able to contribute to defining that report card as you go. This means you assemble a team of people who are capable of quickly pivoting and rolling with the punches, not people who are great at doing what has already been defined for them.

If Simone had the insight skills required of a leader, she would have considered her people needs in the context of her own strengths and weaknesses as a leader. Rather than look for candidates who were considered great at completing tasks and executing like her, she might have interviewed her prospective team members for their ability to be resourceful, for a demonstrated appetite and aptitude for learning on their own and teaching themselves, and for the ability to work autonomously. Simone would have asked interviewees for examples of previous experience taking projects to the next step through initiative and of how they handled setbacks and challenges, how they demonstrated resilience.

Instead, Simone hired people who mirrored her own abilities. They were exceptional at following and executing orders, as she had been as an individual contributor. Yet when she could not clearly define next steps, give specific orders, or make herself available to them to explain the larger context of her requests, her team members were lost and could not perform. Then, rather than offering leadership and righting the situation, she blamed them for their inability to do their job. At the same time, they blamed Simone for her inability to provide adequate direction and for her harsh and debilitating criticism. One by one, she lost her team members, which forced her to rebuild, slowing down the department's ability to deliver to the larger organization. In the end, Simone's inability to lead her team had major implications for her career trajectory and her reputation as a leader.

As we discussed earlier in this book, many people who are outstanding individual contributors arrive at the leadership seat without a playbook for how to manage, coach, and lead other people. When you have an opportunity to take on a leadership role, it is a great time to stop and think about how you see yourself as a leader. What are you good at? What are your strengths? Where are your weaknesses and gaps?

You may want to consider using one of the many leadership assessment tools that exist in the marketplace today. Or think about having a candid conversation with your mentor, who can give you feedback, including the good, bad, and the ugly. They can offer insight into how you have demonstrated leadership skills over the years, how you have matured into a leader, or what you need to address and improve.

When you are blind about who you are as a leader, when you don't understand your gaps and opportunities for growth, and you lack the ability to make changes and adjustments to your leadership style, it will be easy for you to make the wrong choices when recruiting and hiring a team. Without knowing who you are, you will choose the wrong personality types and miss out on the skills you need on a team.

Remember, if your goal is to be a powerful, impactful, and influential leader, you will have to understand and have the ability to lead people with personalities and work styles of all kinds. You will enjoy much more success if you choose a team that complements, not mimics, who you are and your working style. As we discussed earlier in the book, when you step into a leadership role, you will not always have the opportunity to choose your team, but if you do, your insight into yourself and the people who report to you will be extraordinarily helpful.

Still, even if you are skilled at reading and evaluating people, it can be easy to miss an important consideration about a potential employee. Sometimes people must be in the right environment, on the right project, or working with the right manager before you can really see what they are capable of. I have seen many professionals plod along in their careers for years before suddenly, when given the right opportunity with the right leader, they really start to shine. When you are choosing people for roles on your team, look carefully within your organization for people who may not have been given a shot at the challenging, high-profile assignments. If you are an inspiring, fair, and motivating leader, you might be the one who uncovers your company's next superstar.

As an insightful leader, when looking to hire a team, especially if you are interviewing internal candidates, you want to be sure to consider who potential candidates have worked for, what kinds of opportunities they have had, and whether or not they have been tested with challenging "stretch" assignments. Have they been given serious responsibility or the opportunity to show that they can motivate and retain people?

These are all helpful clues in understanding whether the team members you choose will have the ability to innovate, or to support and inspire others to do so, and contribute to an environment where people want to work, learn, and stay. Today's leaders are increasingly becoming responsible not only for getting people to execute a plan but also for retaining the best talent. That can only happen with active engagement, training, and coaching.

As you develop your own insight as a leader, you must pass along what you learn to the future leaders you are responsible for creating. Your job as a leader is to enable your people to do a great job by making sure that they have the technological, financial, and human resources they need to excel. At the same time, you are responsible for empowering them to make decisions, and for teaching them how to advance, pivot, and produce.

LEADERSHIP GEM:

The people you choose to be on your team will be part of your legacy as a leader.

A component of insight is understanding cause and effect within the larger context of a project or direction. Part of your job as a leader is to use insight to understand why certain things happen and what could be done to cause a different outcome . . . in effect, to problem solve. In our fast-paced competitive world, great leaders have the ability to look at what the competition is doing, understand their motivations in the context of the resources they have, and anticipate the competition's next move. Insightful leaders try to think two or three events ahead of what is currently taking place and then invest their own firms' resources to keep pace with or get out ahead of the competition.

Oversight focuses on the here and now of executing a strategy; insight plans and drives toward the future. Oversight focuses on keeping pace with the competition; insight defines the future competitive parameters in the industry and determines the technological advances needed to provide the company with operational leverage.

Sinclair was the president of a small liberal arts school known for its undergraduate programs in biology, chemistry, and scientific research. As the cost of higher education was rising at double-digit rates, many small schools were experiencing a decline in their student population, and Sinclair's school was no exception. Her student population was largely from out of state. Students sought the prestige of earning an undergraduate degree from one of the top schools in the country with a strong reputation for science. Many of the students were also largely first-generation for whom costs were a key consideration when deciding where to go to school.

With new and advanced technology, Sinclair had the opportunity to transfer many of the school's courses from in-person classrooms to an online platform. Many of the school's professors were very willing to leverage the technology and teach students virtually, and this would significantly decrease the cost of attending classes for the students.

Sinclair felt strongly that students preferred the full college experience of living in dorms, eating in dining halls, and participating in sports, clubs, and other campus activities. While this was certainly true for some students, a growing number wanted access to an online experience that could decrease the overall cost associated with attending four to five years of college courses to earn a degree.

However, Sinclair did not believe there would be enough students who wanted an online experience. As a result, she failed to commit any intellectual or experiential resources to considering what a full online or a hybrid (part online and part in-person) classroom experience might look like for students. Nor did she give thought to how the school could leverage resources or potentially use virtual reality to create experiences for students within a twenty-mile radius of their homes.

Then came the global pandemic. Like many workers around the country, students were forced to stay home for a year. Colleges and universities that had already invested in online learning quickly pivoted to expand their class offerings. Other institutions started offering students virtual campus experiences. Schools with scale quickly lowered their pricing on some course offerings and enjoyed a significant influx of students. Many professors looked to join colleges and universities that offered the flexibility to teach many or all courses virtually. Schools, including Sinclair's, that had not invested in technology could not pivot fast enough to attract students. In fact, Sinclair's school lost significant numbers of students to competitors. While the competitor schools did not have the same reputation, their insight about the future of a college experience placed them out ahead of the competition, and by making significant investment in technology, they were able to provide students with a superior virtual experience.

Insight drives leaders to innovate and make decisions about building for the future versus focusing on maintaining what is. Insight helps leaders to decide on the right partners and resources they can leverage to advance market share and outpace competitors.

The dynamic rate of innovation in our world today will continue to drive us all to move faster. Developing sharp insight into what types of innovation the world will require will be key to your ability to be a powerful leader.

FINAL THOUGHTS

The world is moving faster than ever before. The COVID-19 crisis has been one of the truly global experiences in my lifetime; people everywhere have been affected. Professionals have had an opportunity to rethink the value proposition of their careers and their jobs. In many cases the "trust" factor between employer and employee has been redefined, and hybrid work is now here to stay.

Even before this great pandemic, the generational shift on its own was demanding a different kind of leadership, one that was more engaging, empathetic, and egalitarian. The changing demographic was demanding a level of equity and transparency that work environments were, frankly, not ready for.

To lead amidst all this change is challenging. Whether you are a global, multinational leader or you have just started your own company, if you move forward with intention and a strategy, I do believe that the "pearls" in this book will help you to be a more powerful, impactful, and influential leader—one who can *Lead to Win*!

Acknowledgments

I began to get the inspiration for this book in 2018, as I took stock of over thirty years on Wall Street and the leaders who I had met, observed, and learned from. I also considered the professionals who I was spending a lot of time with and who were quickly becoming the dominant population in the workforce: Millennials. I realized, as I listened to their perspectives and counseled them through their challenges, that they had very different expectations of their work environments, and certainly from the people who they reported to, than I had when I started my career. I had the "aha" moment that a different type of leader was required in today's workplace to manage and lead these professionals and emerging leaders. I also realized that I had formed my own thoughts regarding effective leadership that had been gleaned from studying effective and not-so-effective leaders over the course of my career, and that this perspective had attributes that would fit the context we find ourselves in today—and thus, *Lead to Win* was born.

As I express my gratitude for completing this work, I HAVE to start with God is good, all of the time, and all of the time, God is good! I must begin here because I know WHOSE I am. Without HIM, I can do nothing, but through HIM, I can do all things that are mine to do!

As always, I want to thank my terrific agent, Barbara Lowenstein, who gently but effectively nudges me to write, even when I think I have said what I needed to say. I thank you, Barbara, for your impeccable timing.

I thank my writing consigliere, Kellie Tabron, who is always ready to remedy, edit, and prod with new questions, ideas, and corrections. Kellie, it is always fun to collaborate, write, and work with you! Dare I say we do another?

Caroline Sutton, thank you again for believing in the importance of my work and giving me the best compliment ever! I love working with you and your "straight, no chaser" style. A woman after my own heart. It's been a few decades that we have known each other, and I honor the fact that some things don't change, and for that I am grateful!

To Natasha Soto, the newest member of Team Carla, welcome aboard! Thanks for your diligence and help in getting this to the finish line.

To Cal Hunter, you have been my commercial partner in crime since *Expect to Win*! Thanks for investing your professional expertise in helping me to drive the success of both *Expect to Win* and *Strategize to Win* in the Barnes and Noble franchise and beyond. I also thank you for introducing me to your amazing teammate, Jimmy Tu. There is no better combination for executing the impossible and making it look easy. Thank you!

I thank all my mentees, the people whom I have met on the road during my speaking engagements, those who have engaged with me via social media, and leaders who are sitting in leadership seats today. Your courage to share your professional challenges with me has inspired this work, and I honor what you have done. I hope that I make you proud.

To my number one, Victor Franklin, thank you for the support and the "atta girl"s. I appreciate and cherish you.

To the avid readers of *Expect to Win* and *Strategize to Win*, thanks for making the investment of your time to read these works, for sharing the "pearls" with others, and for all of your support. This book would not have happened without you.